Contents

Inhaltsverzeichnis

Table des matières

Traditional japanese small motif and medium-sized motif patterns

Kamon Yoshimoto

The patterns called KOMON (small patterns) in this book are the "small patterns" which were simply used for decorating the surface of such things as clothes and patterned papers or other industrially produced objects of art as well as daily utensils, i.e. colourful small patterns composed by means of collecting or distributing minute motifs as seen on EDO KOMON KIRE (cloth with small patterns).

The CHUGATA - MON (medium-sized patterns) in this book do not represent large flowers or birds as seen in YUZEN patterns, but rather, refer to patterns larger than the above-mentioned small patterns, that is, patterns of medium size.

SARASA patterns and SHIMA (stripes) patterns were imported from abroad and were assimilated into Japanese culture. The KOMON patterns, however, are absolutely typical Japanese patterns created and developed without being affected by foreign influence. These KOMONS (small patterns) first came into existence at the beginning of the Edo period (1604-1867). Their history reaches back over more than 300 years.

The small patterns were first developed in Edo for the complete dress of the Samurai classes (KAMISHIMO). These unique patterns were habitually worn by the various feudal lords of the day. Specific patterns were reserved for the exclusive use of the DAIMYO (feudal lords) and were not allowed to be worn by the common people.

However, in the second half of the Edo period when peace reigned over the land, the power of the common people had increased, and these KOMONS (small patterns) which had been monopolized by the Samurai were used by the common people, too. Various unique patterns were created and their use spread to the general public with the exception of the Tomegara pattern exclusively used by the feudal lords.

The patterns themselves were inspired by a wide variety of numerous motifs, derived from natural phenomena such as hail, rain, etc., and seasonal as well as environmental elements. A collection of the chief 64 patterns of this type can be found on pages 8 to 11 of this book.

The small patterns first became popular among the townfolks for use in their clothing. Gradually they came into use in the Kabuki world, creating new fashions with elegant versions of KOMONS (small patterns) and CHUGATA patterns.

In the meantime, patterned papers designed from pictures taken of the wadded silk garments worn by actors, and papers printed with KOMON motifs met with women's approval. These patterns were also used for changeable paper-doll clothes, for toys made from pictured paper or Chiyo-gamis (papers with gay-coloured pictures) and used as patterns for work pieces and small objects for the enjoyment of the masses.

This literature was compiled and printed with the purpose and in the hope of preserving the history of KOMON patterns which flourished during the time of our predecessors and were popular especially among the general public. Since the end of World War II, the use of traditional patterns has begun to decline rapidly. Therefore, in order to preserve the patterns, it is our intention to publish a reproduced version of the KOMON patterns with a modern touch so that the reader might acquire a better understanding of their uniqueness and in the hope that they might influence modern decorative design.

This book contains the following five categories, with a total of over 900 different patterns.

1. EDO - KOMON (small patterns of the Edo period) (cloth) 125 patterns
2. KOMON of the Meiji and Taisho periods (cloth) 369 patterns
3. Arts and crafts paper (small motif) 72 patterns
4. CHUGATA patterns (medium-sized motifs) of the Meiji and Taisho periods (cloth) 111 patterns
5. CHUGATA patterns (medium-sized motifs) of the Edo, Meiji and Taisho periods (paper) 239 patterns

Total of 916 patterns

Traditionelle japanische kleine Muster und mittelgroße Muster

Kamon Yoshimoto

Bei den Mustern, die in diesem Buch mit KOMON (kleine Muster) bezeichnet werden, handelt es sich um die „kleinen Muster", die zur Verzierung von Kleidungsstücken, Bastelpapier oder sonstigen industriell gefertigen kunstgewerblichen Gegenständen sowie Gegenständen des täglichen Gebrauchs dienen. Es sind farbige kleine Muster, die durch Kombination oder Verteilung winziger Elemente, wie bei EDO KOMON KIRE (kleingemusterter Stoff), entstehen.

Die in diesem Heft gezeigten CHU-GATA-MON (mittelgroße Muster) stellen keine großen Blumen oder Vögel wie bei den YUZEN - Mustern dar; es handelt sich um eher größere Muster im Vergleich zu den oben beschriebenen kleinen Mustern.

Die SARASA- und SHIMA - Muster (SHIMA = Streifen) stammen ursprünglich aus dem Ausland, sind aber von der japanischen Kultur assimiliert worden. Bei den KOMON-Mustern handelt es sich jedoch um ganz typische japanische Muster, die ohne ausländischen Einfluß entstanden sind und weiterentwickelt wurden. Die KOMONS (kleine Muster) sind nach Beginn der Edozeit (1604-1867) entstanden. Ihre Geschichte reicht mehr als 300 Jahre zurück.

Die kleinen Muster hatten ihren Ausgangspunkt in Edo, wo sie für die Kleidung der Samuraiklasse (KAMISHIMO) entwickelt wurden. Diese einzigartigen Muster wurden in jenen Tagen gewöhnlich von den verschiedenen Feudalherren verwendet. Bestimmte Muster waren den DAIMYO (Feudalherren) vorbehalten und nicht für das einfache Volk bestimmt.

In der zweiten Hälfte der Edozeit, als Frieden im Land herrschte, nahm die Macht des Volkes zu und diese KOMONS (kleinen Muster), welche die Samuraiklasse als ihr Eigentum betrachtete, wurden nun auch vom Volk benutzt. Dabei entstanden zahlreiche einzigartige Muster, die in der gesamten Bevölkerung Verbreitung fanden. Die einzige Ausnahme bildete das Tomegara (besonderes Muster) der Feudalherren.

Bei den Mustern selbst sind der Phantasie keine Grenzen gesetzt, sie orientieren sich an Naturereignissen wie Hagel, Regen usw., an jahreszeitlichen Elementen sowie an Elementen aus der Umwelt. Auf den Seiten 8 bis 11 dieses Buchs sind die 64 wichtigsten Muster dargestellt.

Die kleinen Muster erfreuten sich zunächst bei der Stadtbevölkerung großer Beliebtheit, die sie für ihre Kleidung benutzte. Nach und nach erreichten sie auch die japanische Theaterwelt (Kabuki - Theater), wo sie als elegante Version der KOMONS (kleine Muster) und der CHUGATA - Muster eine neue Mode schufen.

Zur gleichen Zeit begann man damit, die Muster auf der wattierten Seidenkleidung japanischer Schauspieler von Abbildungen zu übernehmen und diese auf Papier zu drucken. Dieses Papier sowie mit kleinen KOMONS bedrucktes Papier wurde bei den Frauen immer beliebter. Außerdem ging man immer mehr dazu über, aus dieser Art von Papier auch Wechselkleidung für Anziehpuppen, mit Bildern versehenes Papierspielzeug oder Chiyogamis (Papier mit farbenfrohen Mustern) herzustellen. Diese wurden insbesondere zum Bekleben von kleineren kunstgewerblichen Gegenständen benutzt und erfreuten sich beim Volk großer Beliebtheit.

Diese Informationen wurden zusammengestellt und gedruckt, um die Geschichte des KOMON - Musters zu bewahren, das bei unseren Vorfahren eine Blütezeit erlebte und vor allem beim Volk weit verbreitet war. Nach dem Ende des Zweiten Weltkriegs gerieten traditionelle Muster schnell in Vergessenheit. Um die Muster zu bewahren, war es daher unsere Absicht, eine Reproduktion der KOMON - Muster in modernem Stil zu veröffentlichen, so daß der Leser ihre Einzigartigkeit besser zu schätzen lernt. Außerdem hoffen wir, daß sie Einfluß auf modernes Design ausüben mögen.

Dieses Buch umfaßt die fünf folgenden Kategorien mit insgesamt über 900 verschiedenen Mustern.

1. EDO-KOMON (kleine Muster aus der Edozeit) (Stoff) 125 Muster
2. KOMON aus der Meidschi- und Taishozeit (Stoff) 369 Muster
3. Bastelpapier (kleine Muster) 72 Muster
4. CHUGATA - Muster (mittelgroße Muster) aus der Meidschi- und Taishozeit (Stoff) 111 Muster
5. CHUGATA - Muster (mittelgroße Muster) aus der Edo-, Meidschi- und Taishozeit (Papier) 239 Muster

Gesamt 916 Muster

Petits motifs traditionnels japonais et motifs de taille moyenne

Kamon Yoshimoto

Dans ce livre, les motifs appelés KOMON (petits motifs) sont des «petits motifs» destinés à orner des objets comme les vêtements, les patrons, ou encore des objets d'art industriels, de même que des ustensiles quotidiens. Ce sont de petits motifs colorés, formés en combinant et en répartissant de très petits motifs comme sur le EDO KOMON KIRE (tissu à petits motifs).

Les CHUGATA - MON (motifs de taille moyenne) de ce livre, ne représentent pas de larges fleurs ni des oiseaux comme sur les modèles YUZEN, mais plutôt des motifs un peu plus grands que les petits motifs cités ci-dessus.

Les motifs SARASA et SHIMA (rayures) ont été importés de l'étranger et assimilés à la culture japonaise. Cependant, les motifs KOMON sont typiquement japonais, créés et développés sans aucune influence étrangère. Ces KOMON (petits motifs) sont apparus après le début de l'ère Edo (1604-1867), ce qui signifie que leur histoire est vieille de plus de 300 ans.

A l'origine, les petits motifs ont été développés dans l'ère Edo, pour les tenues de cérémonie des Samouraï (KAMISHIMO). Ces motifs exceptionnels étaient habituellement utilisés par différents seigneurs féodaux de cette époque. Certains motifs étaient spécialement réservés aux DAÏMYO (seigneurs féodaux) et non destinés au peuple.

Dans la deuxième moitié de l'ère Edo la paix régnait dans tout le pays, le pouvoir du peuple avait pris de l'importance, et ces KOMONS (petits motifs), qui étaient la propriété des Samouraï, commençaient à être utilisés également par le peuple. De nombreux motifs uniques firent leur apparition et se répandirent très vite dans le peuple. Seule exception, le Tomegara, motif exclusivement utilisé par les seigneurs féodaux.

Les motifs eux-mêmes sont variés dans les dessins et basés sur des phénomènes naturels tels que la grêle, la pluie, etc., des éléments de saison et d'environnement. Les 64 motifs les plus importants sont réunis dans les pages 8 à 11 de ce livre.

Les petits motifs sont tout d'abord devenus populaires auprès des citadins qui s'en servaient pour leurs habits. Petit à petit, ils ont également atteint le monde du théâtre japonais (théâtre Kabuki), pour lancer une nouvelle mode avec une version plus élégante des motifs KOMONS (petits motifs) et CHUGATA.

Entretemps, le papier à motifs reprenant les dessins des vêtements en soie capitonnée des acteurs japonais et les petits motifs KOMON teintés étaient très appréciés par les femmes. Ces motifs étaient aussi utilisés pour les habits de poupée en papier et pour les jouets. Le CHIYOGAMIS (papier à motifs gais et colorés) était utilisé pour les petits objets de décoration.

Cette documentation a été compilée et publiée dans le but et l'espoir de préserver l'histoire des motifs KOMON, ayant connu une apogée et étant très répandus chez nos ancêtres. Après la 2nde guerre mondiale, les motifs traditionnels ont été rapidement oubliés. Notre intention était, avec la publication du motif KOMON dans un style plus moderne, de préserver celui-ci et de faire apprécier à nos lecteurs son unicité. Nous espérons aussi qu'il aura quelque influence sur le design moderne.

Ce livre comprend les cinq catégories suivantes, avec au total plus de 900 motifs différents.

1. EDO - KOMON (petits motifs de l'ère Edo) (tissu) 125 motifs
2. KOMON des ères Meïji et Taisho (tissu) 369 motifs
3. Papier dessin (petit motif) 72 motifs
4. Motifs CHUGATA (motifs de taille moyenne) dës ères Meïji et Taisho (tissu) 111 motifs
5. Motifs CHUGATA (motifs de taille moyenne) des èreš Edo, Meïji et Taisho (papier) 239 motifs

Total 916 motifs

List of
KOMON patterns

Übersicht über die
KOMON - Muster

Liste des
motifs KOMON

Shimazu pattern
Shimazu - Muster
Motif Shimazu

Fish scales pattern
Schuppenmuster
Dessin en forme d'écaille

"Water chestnut"
„Wasserkastanie"
«Châtaigne d'eau»

"Seven treasures"
„Sieben Schätze"
«Sept trésors»

"Chrysanthemum blossoms"
„Chrysanthemenblüten"
«Fleurs de chrysanthèmes»

Gourd pattern
Kürbismuster
Motif de potiron

"Hail"
„Hagel"
«Grêle»

"Halved pears"
„Birnenhälften"
«Moitiés de poires»

Whale pattern
Walfischmuster
Dessin de baleine

"Quail in the brook"
„Wachteln im Bauch"
«Caille au ruisseau»

Japanese T - pattern
Japanisches T - Muster
Motif japonais en T

Shokko pattern
Shokko - Muster
Motif Shokko

"Sea cucumber"
„Seegurke"
«Concombre de mer»

Japanese sign for "1"
Japanisches Zeichen für „1"
Motif «Caractère 1»

"Many treasures"
„Viele Schätze"
«Nombreux trésors»

"Small cherry blossoms"
„Kleine Kirschblüten"
«Petites fleurs de cerise»

Ugizawa pattern
Ugizawa - Muster
Motif Ugizawa

"Distant mountains"
„Berge in weiter Ferne"
«Montagnes lointaines»

Chessboard pattern
Schachbrettmuster
Motif échiquier

Hijiki pattern
Hijiki - Muster
Motif Hijiki

Futatsuwari - Togusa pattern
Futatsuwari - Togusa-Muster
Motif Futatsuwari - Togusa

Cross pattern
Kreuzmuster
Motif en forme de croix

"Spinning tops"
„Kreisel"
«Toupies»

Thread-like stripes
Fadenförmige Streifen
Lignes ressemblant à des fils

"Spilt ink"
„Ausgeschüttete Tusche"
«Encre de Chine renversée»

"Sword sheaths"
„Scheiden für Schwerter"
«Gaines d'épée»

"Chrysanthemums and stork nests"
„Chrysanthemen und Storchennester"
«Chrysanthèmes et nids de cigognes»

"Lattice pattern" Go - Hirabishi
„Gittermuster" Go - Hirabishi
«Motif quadrillé» Go - Hirabishi

"Woven mat"
„Geflochtene Matte"
«Tissu en natte»

"Washed-out stripes"
„Verwischte Streifen"
«Rayures effacées»

"Small cherry blossoms"
„Kleine Kirschblüten"
«Petites fleurs de cerise»

"Broken lines"
„Durchbrochene Fäden"
«Lignes rompues»

9

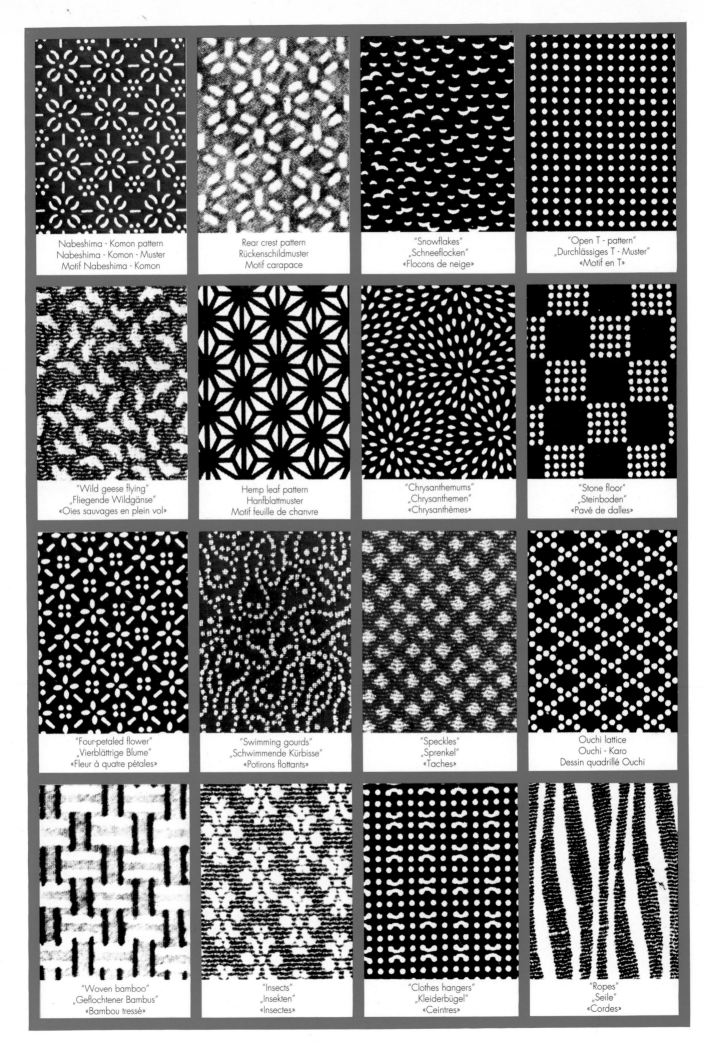

Nabeshima - Komon pattern
Nabeshima - Komon - Muster
Motif Nabeshima - Komon

Rear crest pattern
Rückenschildmuster
Motif carapace

"Snowflakes"
„Schneeflocken"
«Flocons de neige»

"Open T - pattern"
„Durchlässiges T - Muster"
«Motif en T»

"Wild geese flying"
„Fliegende Wildgänse"
«Oies sauvages en plein vol»

Hemp leaf pattern
Hanfblattmuster
Motif feuille de chanvre

"Chrysanthemums"
„Chrysanthemen"
«Chrysanthèmes»

"Stone floor"
„Steinboden"
«Pavé de dalles»

"Four-petaled flower"
„Vierblättrige Blume"
«Fleur à quatre pétales»

"Swimming gourds"
„Schwimmende Kürbisse"
«Potirons flottants»

"Speckles"
„Sprenkel"
«Taches»

Ouchi lattice
Ouchi - Karo
Dessin quadrillé Ouchi

"Woven bamboo"
„Geflochtener Bambus"
«Bambou tressé»

"Insects"
„Insekten"
«Insectes»

"Clothes hangers"
„Kleiderbügel"
«Ceintres»

"Ropes"
„Seile"
«Cordes»

"Peonies" „Pfingstrosen" «Pivoines»	"Feather balls" „Federbälle" «Volants»

"Feather balls and fans"
„Federbälle und Fächer"
«Volants et éventails»

Takedabishi lattice
Takedabishi - Karo
Motif quadrillé Takedabishi

"Shaded plums"
„Pflaumen im Schatten"
«Prunes dans l'ombre»

Triangles
Dreiecke
Triangles

"Chrysanthemums"
„Chrysanthemen"
«Chrysanthèmes»

Chessboard pattern from Okina
Karomuster von Okina
Motif quadrillé d'Okina

Shell pattern
Muschelmuster
Motif coquille

"Ropes"
„Seile"
«Cordes»

Omenami pattern
Omenami-Muster
Motif Omenami

Straw mat pattern
Strohmattenmuster
Motif natte de paille

Japanese sign for "10"
Japanisches Muster für „10"
Motif «Caractère 10»

"Latticed ropes"
„Seile in Gitterform"
«Cordes en forme de quadrillage»

"Crosses"
„Kreuze"
«Croix»

Gourd pattern
Kürbismuster
Motif potiron

Examples of KOMON and TEBIKAECHO patterns (KOMON pattern book)
Beispiele für KOMON- und TEBIKAECHO - Muster (KOMON - Musterheft)
Exemples de motifs KOMON et TEBIKAECHO (Cahier d'échantillons KOMON)

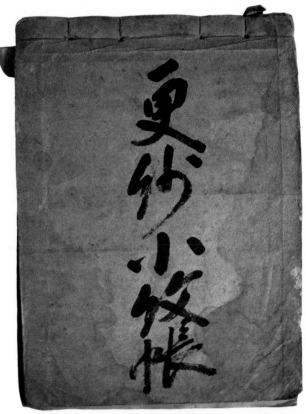

Pattern book of KOMON patterns for Sarasa paper
End of the Edo period
In possession of the Kaikoretsu Institute

Musterheft für Sarasa - Papier mit KOMON - Mustern
Ende der Edozeit
Im Besitz des Kaikoretsu - Instituts

Livre de motifs pour papier Sarasa avec les motifs
KOMON
Fin de l'ère Edo
En possession de l'Institut Kaikoretsu

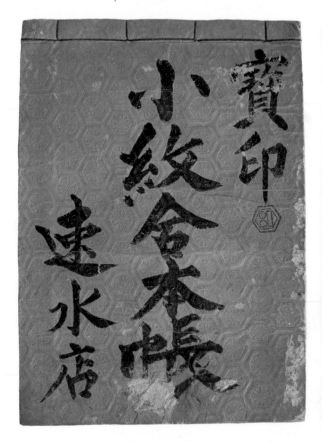

KOMON pattern books
Beginning of the Meiji period
In possession of the Kaikoretsu Institute

KOMON - Musterhefte
Beginn der Meidschizeit
Im Besitz des Kaikoretsu - Instituts

Livres de motifs KOMON
Début de l'ère Meïji
En possession de l'Institut Kaikoretsu

Pattern book for patterned arts and crafts paper
Beginning of the Meiji period
In possession of the Kaikoretsu Institute

Musterheft für Bastelpapiere
Beginn der Meidschizeit
Im Besitz des Kaikoretsu - Instituts

Livre de motifs pour papier dessin
Début de l'ère Meïji
En possession de l'Institut Kaikoretsu

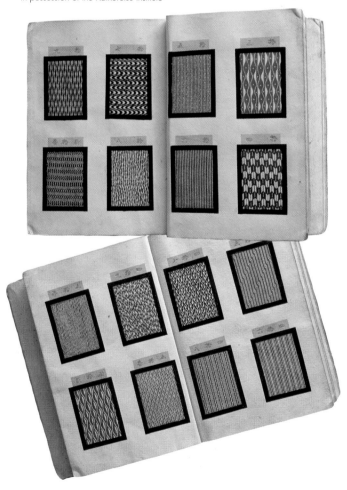

Original print in KOMON - SHIMA colours
Middle of the Meiji period
In possession of the Kaikoretsu Institute

Originaldruck in KOMON-SHIMA-Farben
Mitte der Meidschizeit
Im Besitz des Kaikoretsu - Instituts

Imprimé d'origine aux couleurs KOMON - SHIMA
Milieu de l'ère Meïji
En possession de l'Institut Kaikoretsu

13

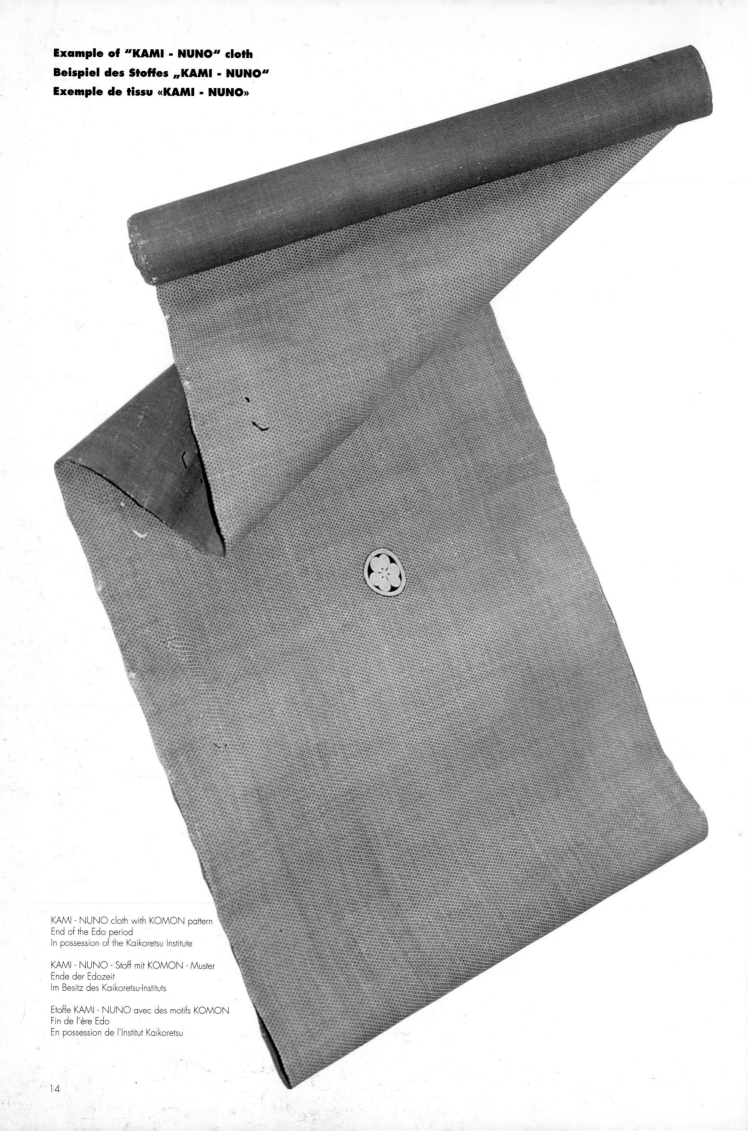

Example of "KAMI - NUNO" cloth
Beispiel des Stoffes „KAMI - NUNO"
Exemple de tissu «KAMI - NUNO»

KAMI - NUNO cloth with KOMON pattern
End of the Edo period
In possession of the Kaikoretsu Institute

KAMI - NUNO - Stoff mit KOMON - Muster
Ende der Edozeit
Im Besitz des Kaikoretsu-Instituts

Etoffe KAMI - NUNO avec des motifs KOMON
Fin de l'ère Edo
En possession de l'Institut Kaikoretsu

14

EDO - KOMON

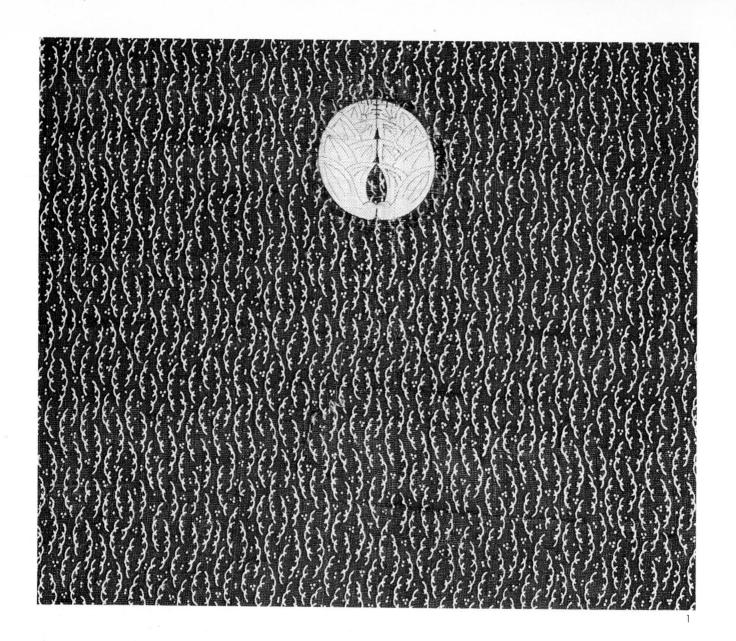

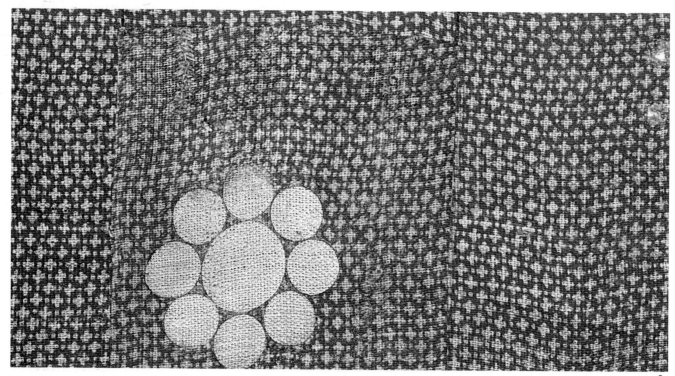

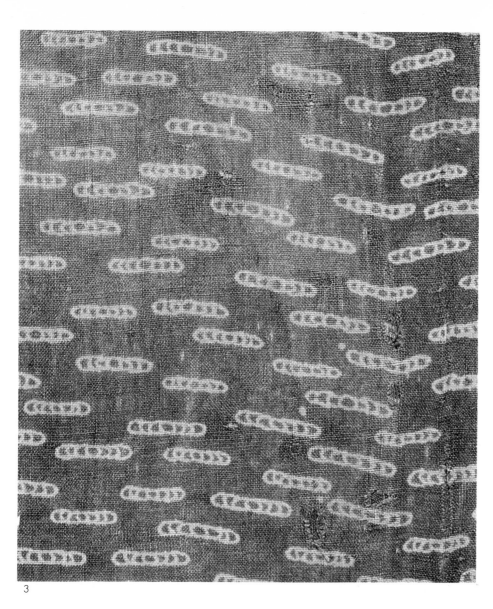

3

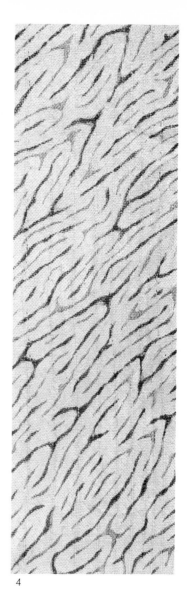

4

5

6

7

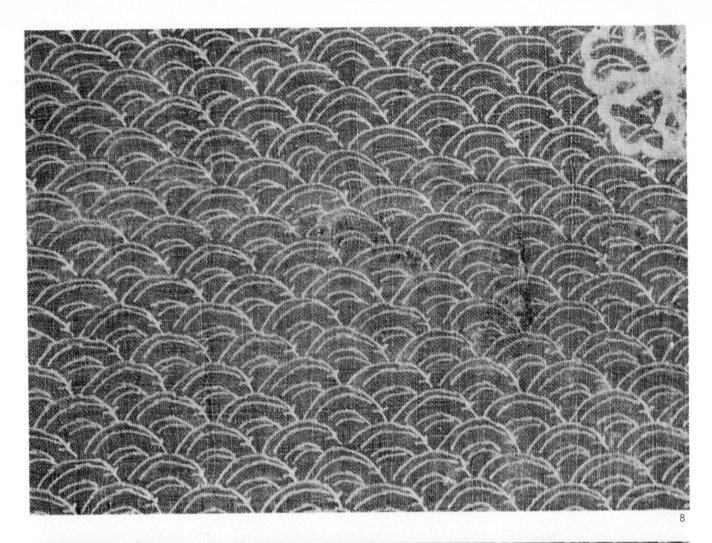

8

9

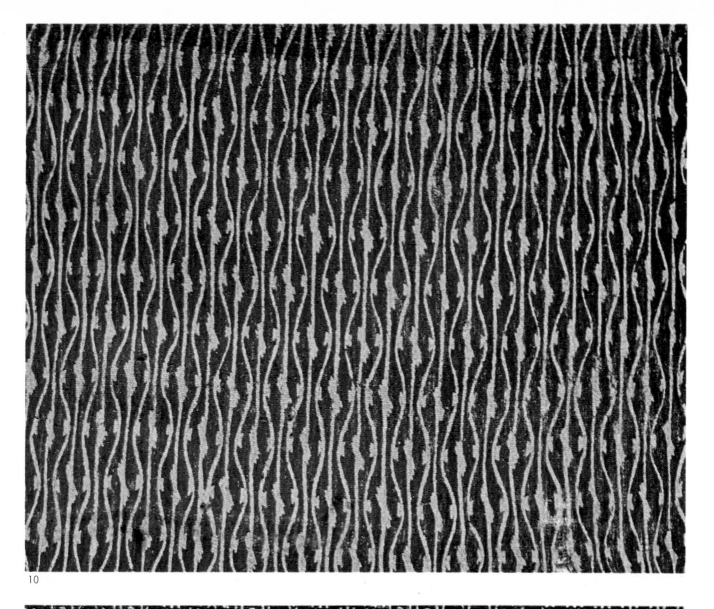

10

11

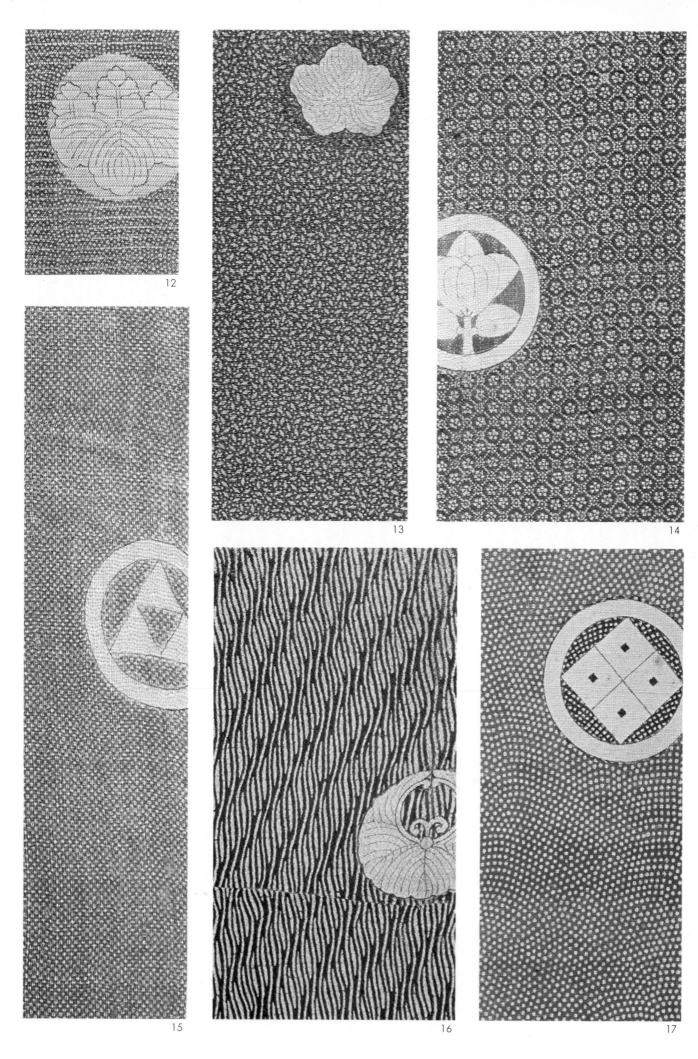

12

13

14

15

16

17

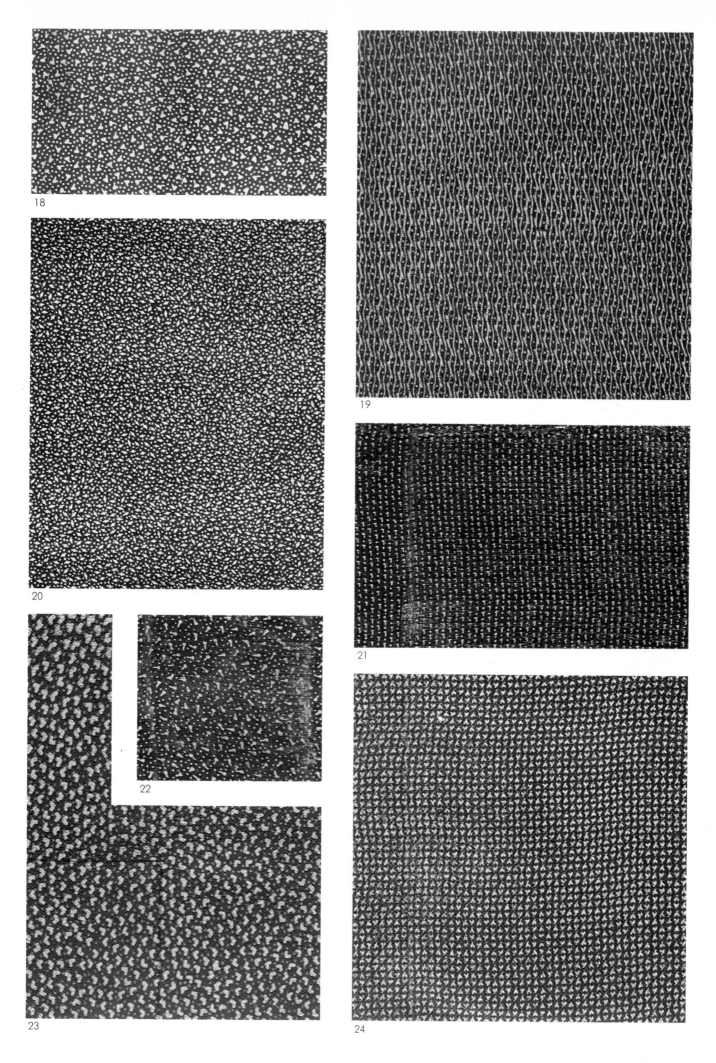

18

19

20

21

22

23

24

25

26

27

28

29

30

31

32

33

34

35

36

37

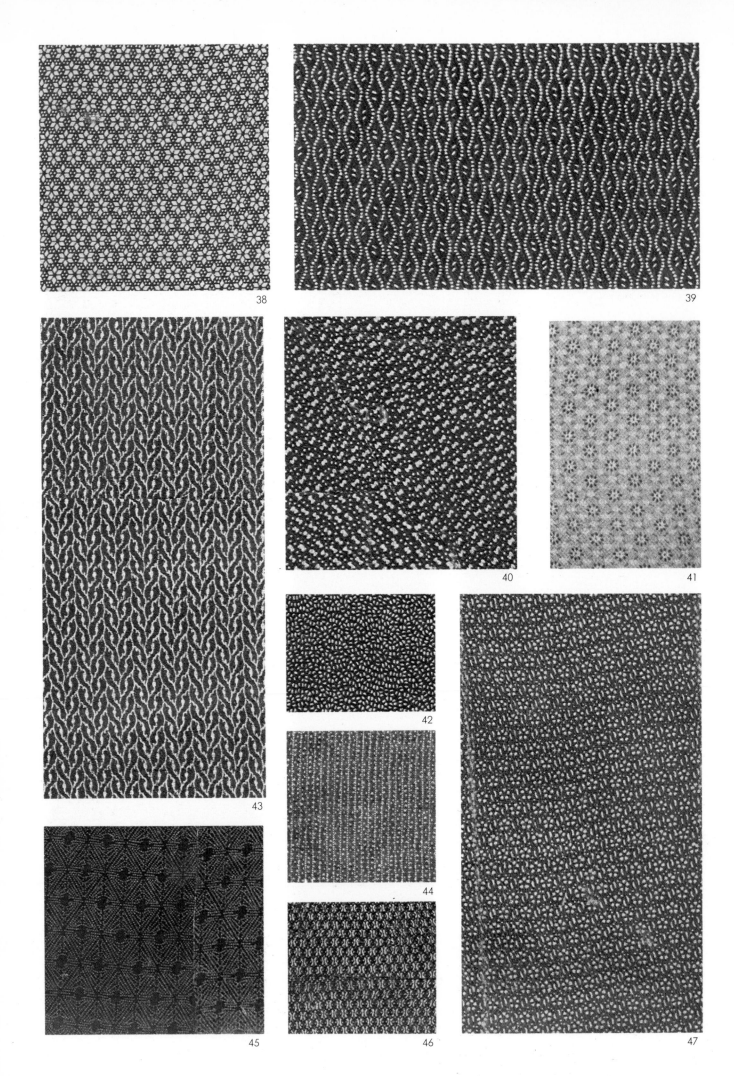

48

49

50

51

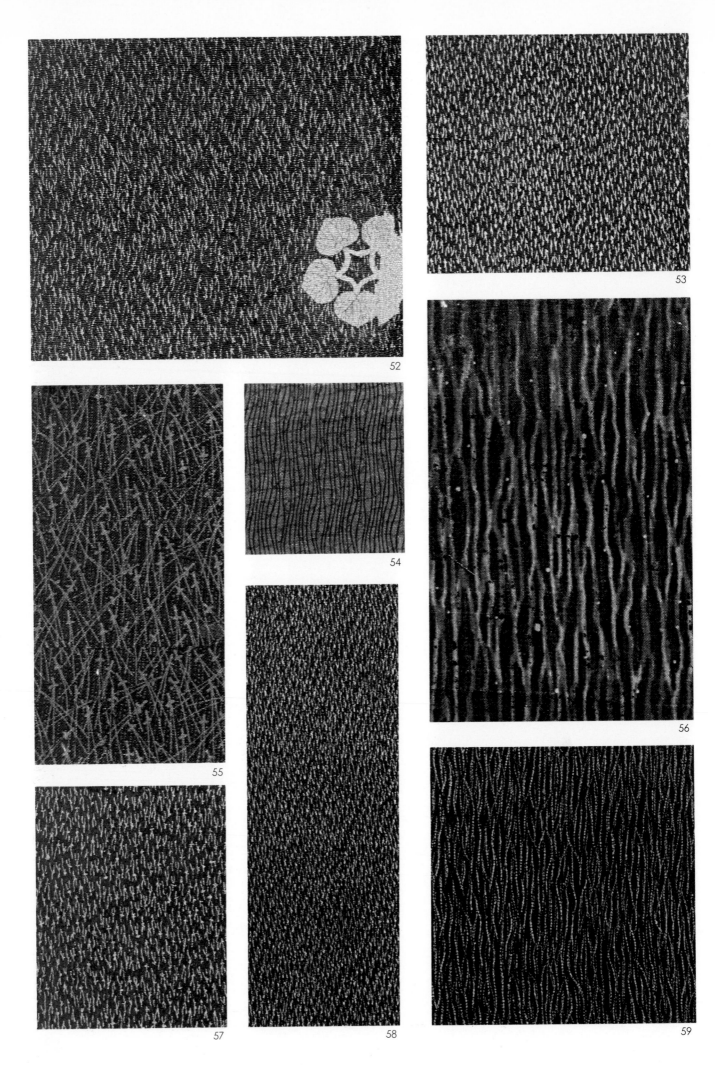

52

53

54

55

56

57

58

59

60

61

62

63

64

65

66

67

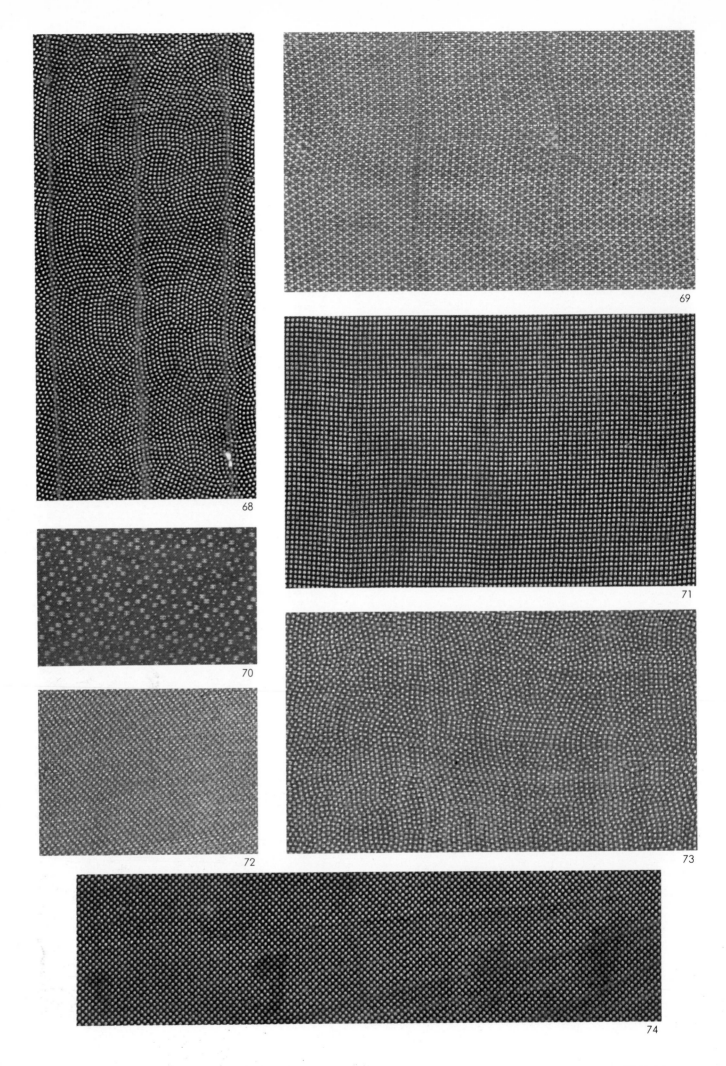

68

69

70

71

72

73

74

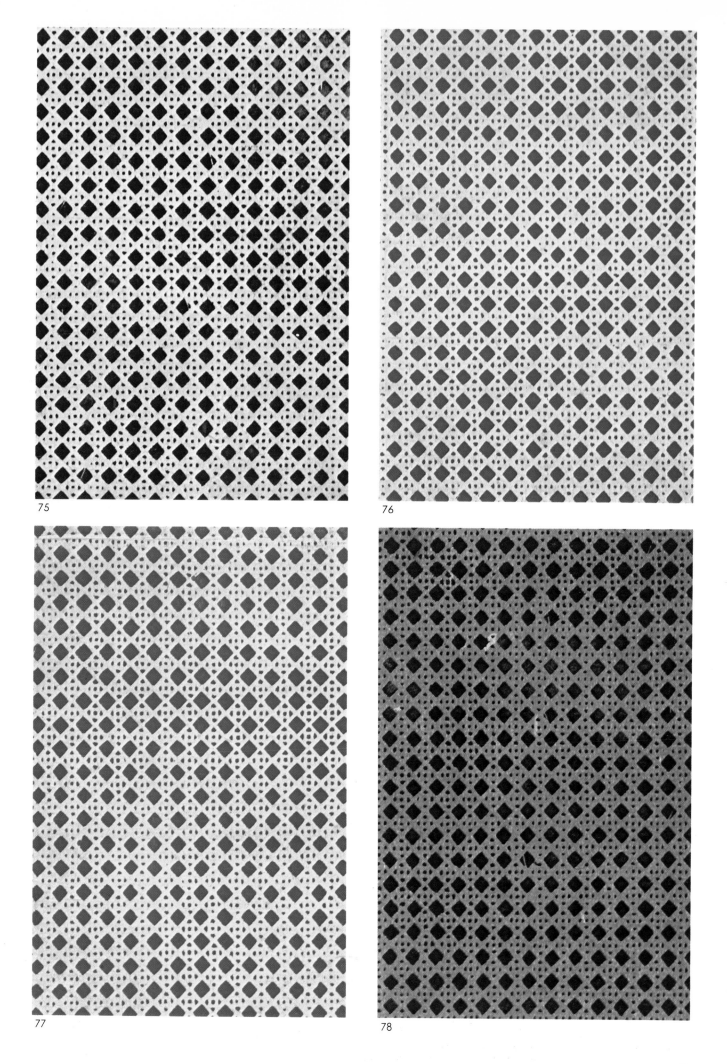

75

76

77

78

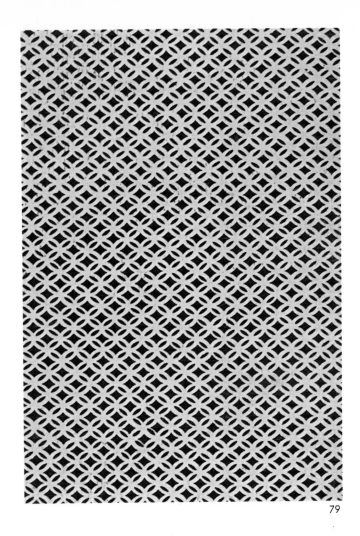

79

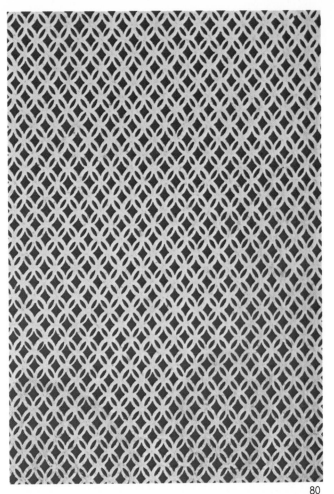

80

81

82

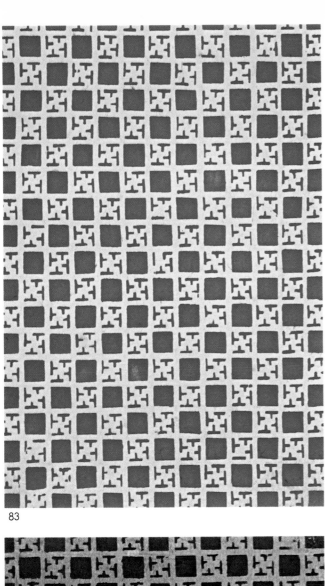

83

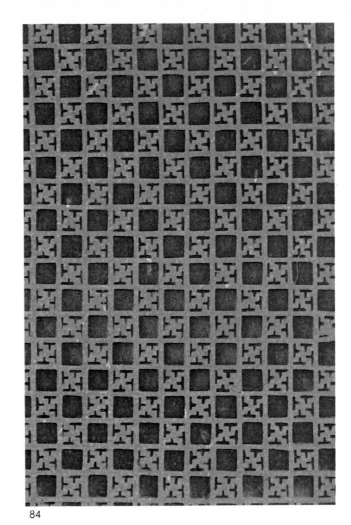

84

85

86

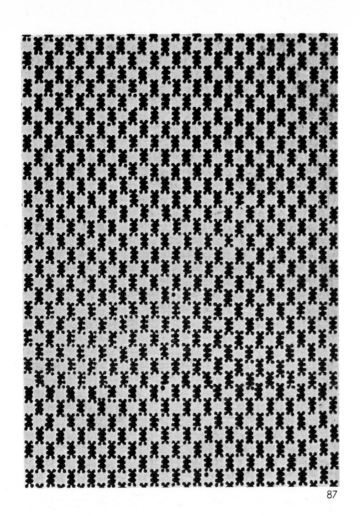

87

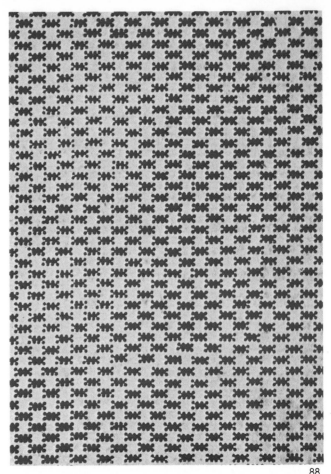

88

89

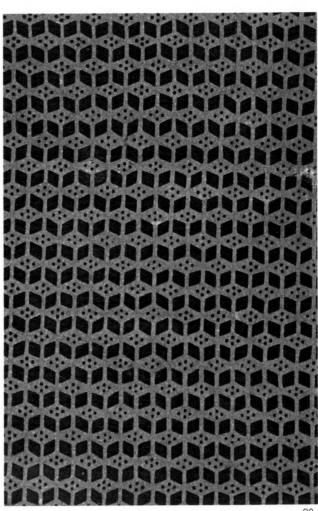

90

91

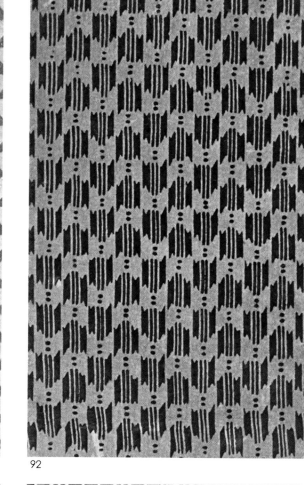

92

93

94

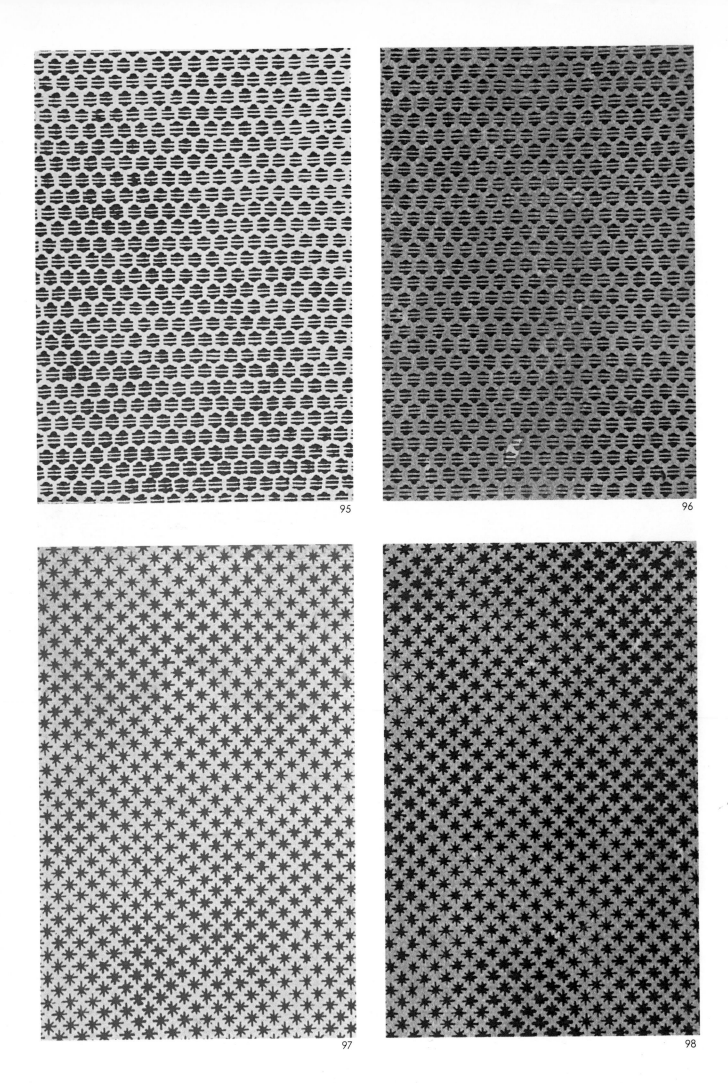

95

96

97

98

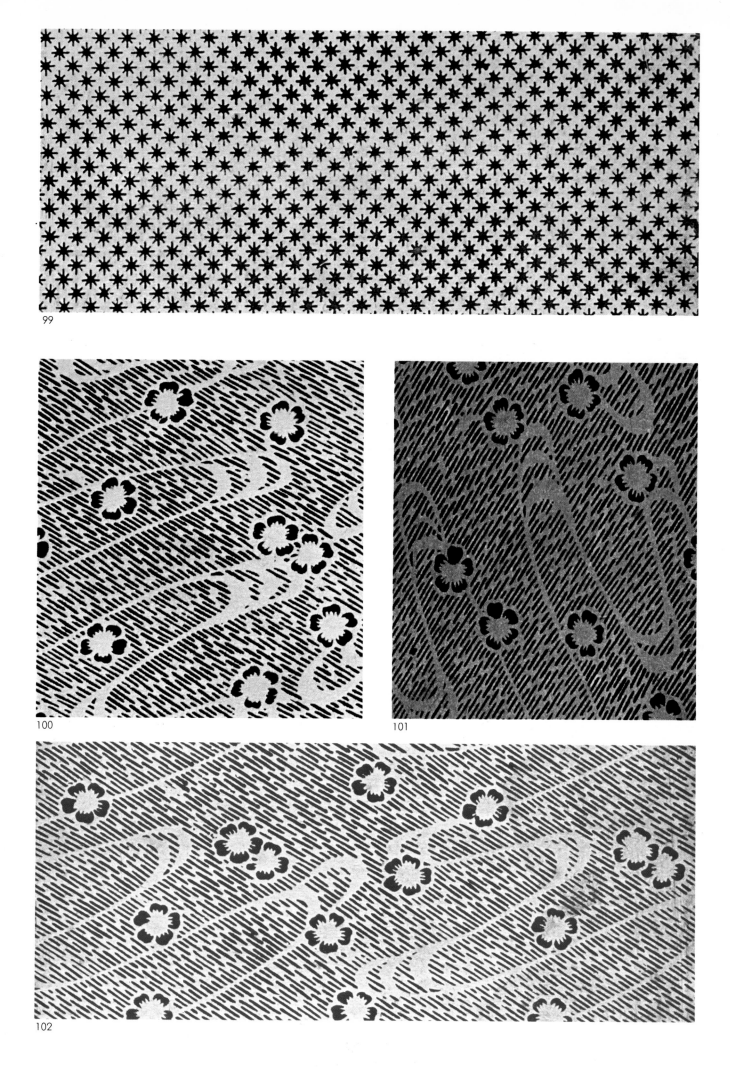

99

100

101

102

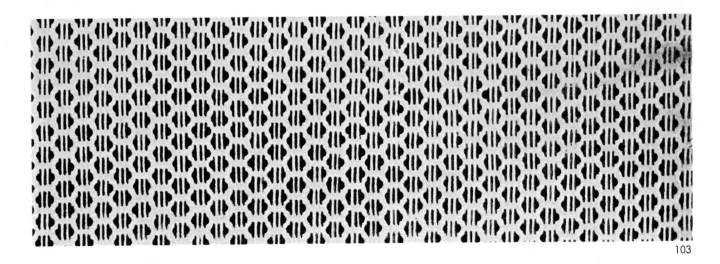

103

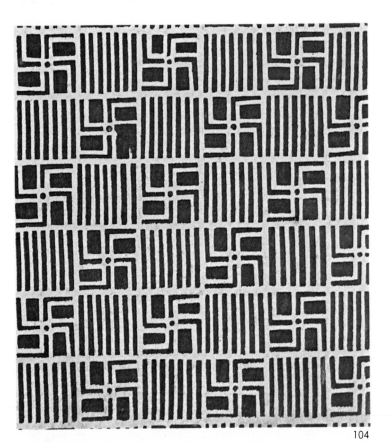

104

105

106

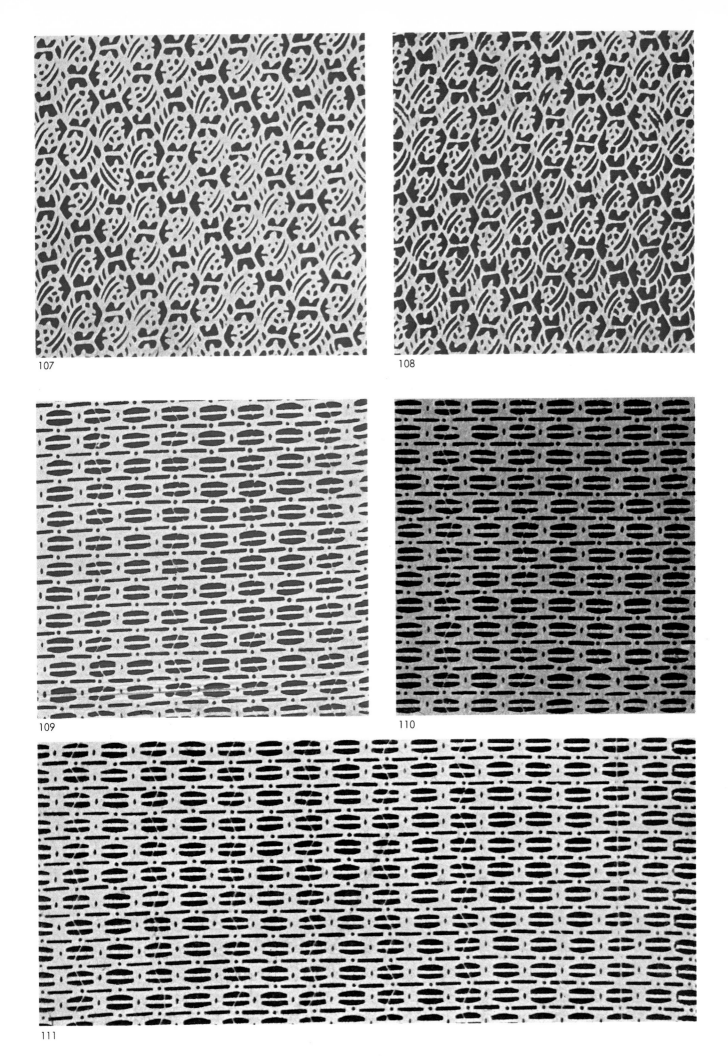

107

108

109

110

111

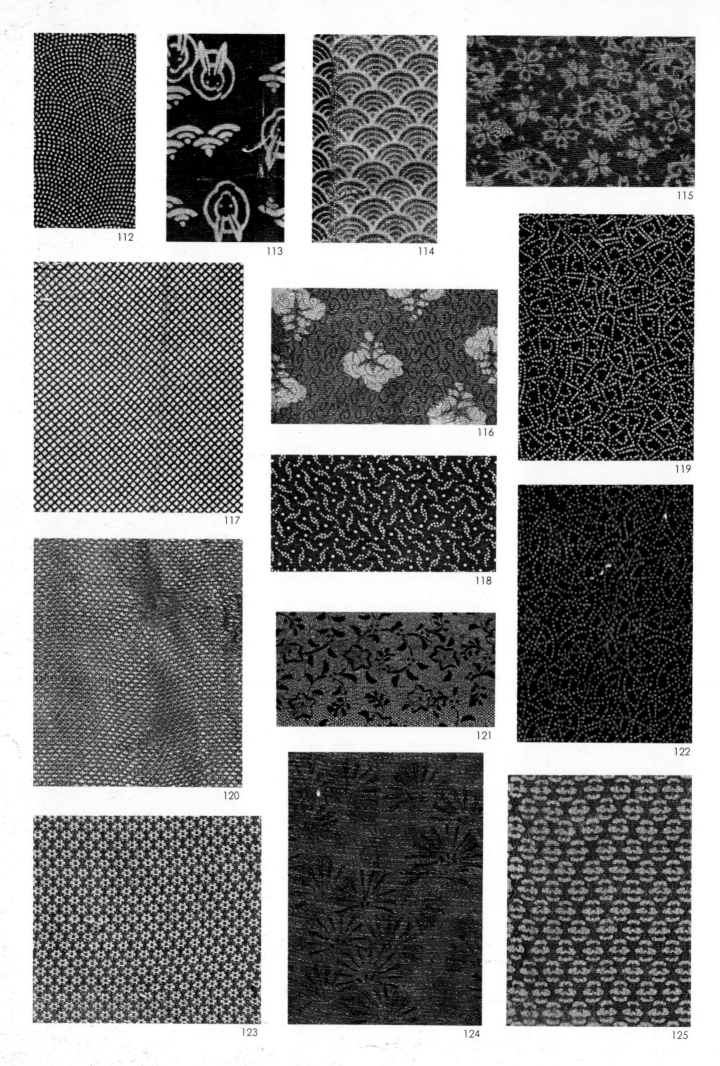

112

113

114

115

116

117

118

119

120

121

122

123

124

125

38

KOMON
of the Meiji and Taisho periods (cloth)

KOMON
aus der Meidschi- und Taishozeit (Stoff)

KOMON
des ères Meïji et Taisho (tissu)

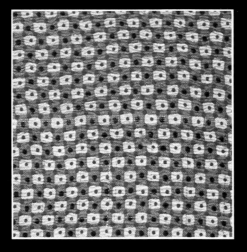

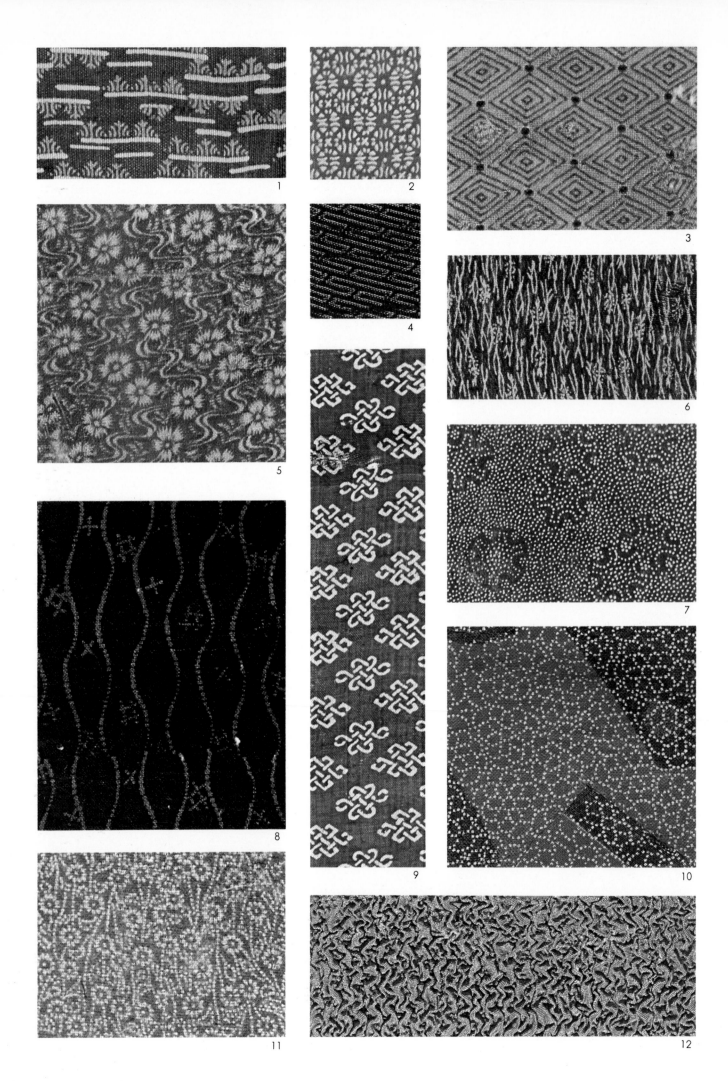

13

14

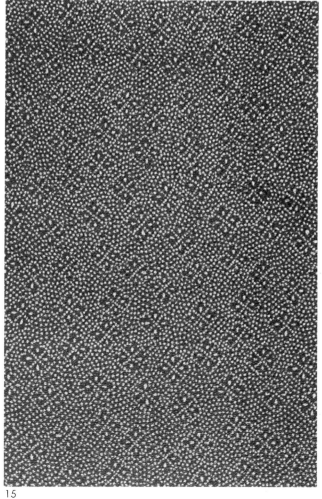

15

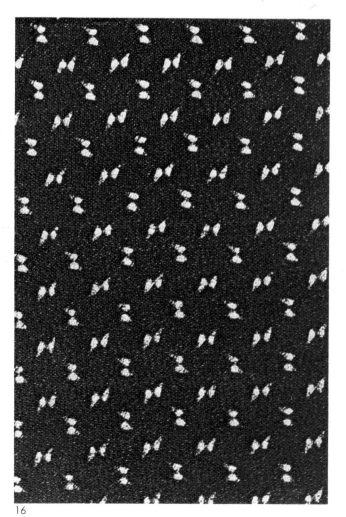

16

25

26

27

28

29

30

31

32

33

34

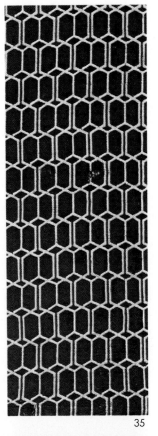

35

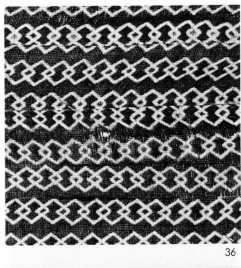

36

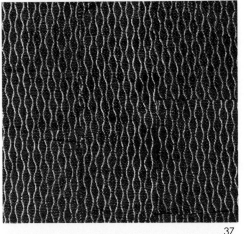

37

38

40

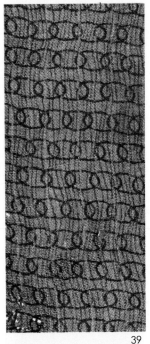

39

41

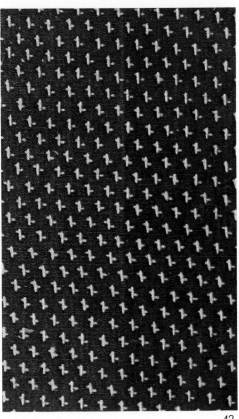

42

43

44

45

46

47

48

49

50

51

52

53

54

55

56

57

58

59

60

61

62

63

64

65

66

67

46

68

69

70

71

72

73

74

75

76

77

78

79

80

81

82

83

84

85

86

87

48

88

89

90

91

92

93

94

95

96

97

98

99

100

101

102

103

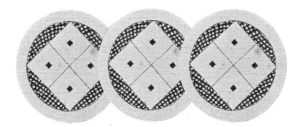

104

105

106

107

108

109

110

111

112

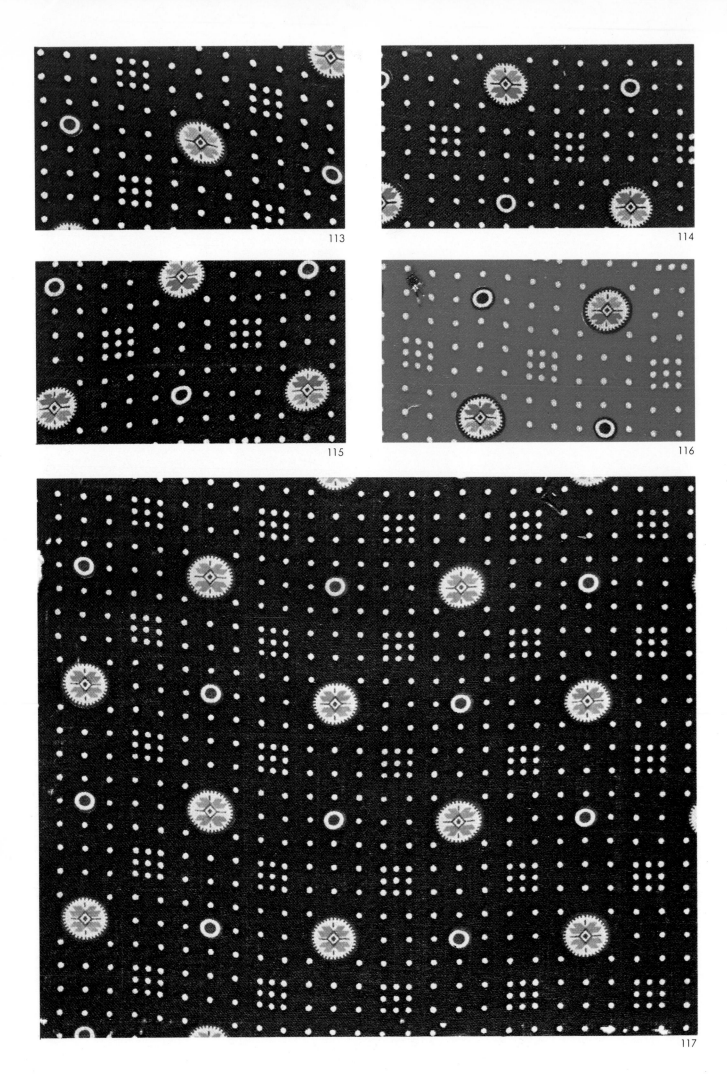

113

114

115

116

117

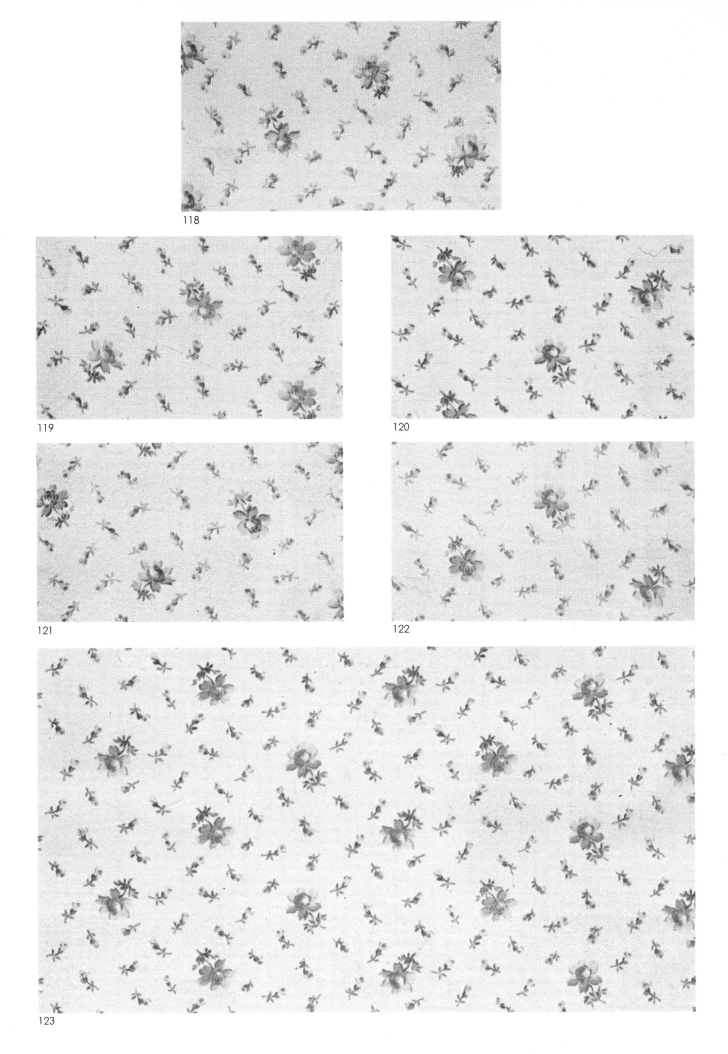

118

119

120

121

122

123

124

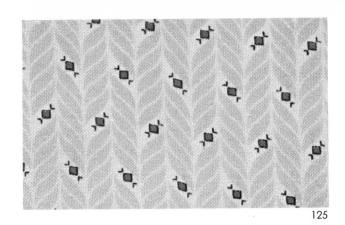

125

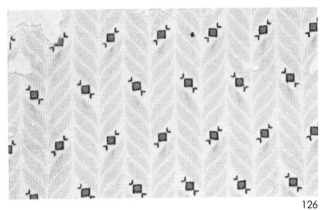

126

127

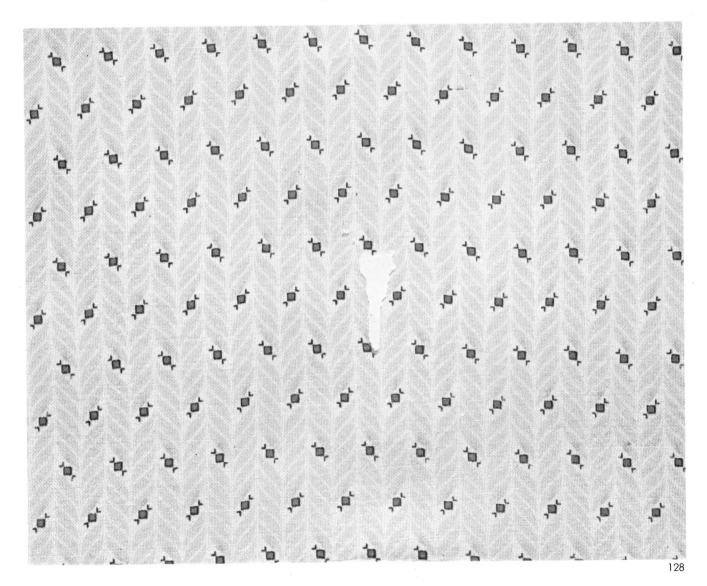

128

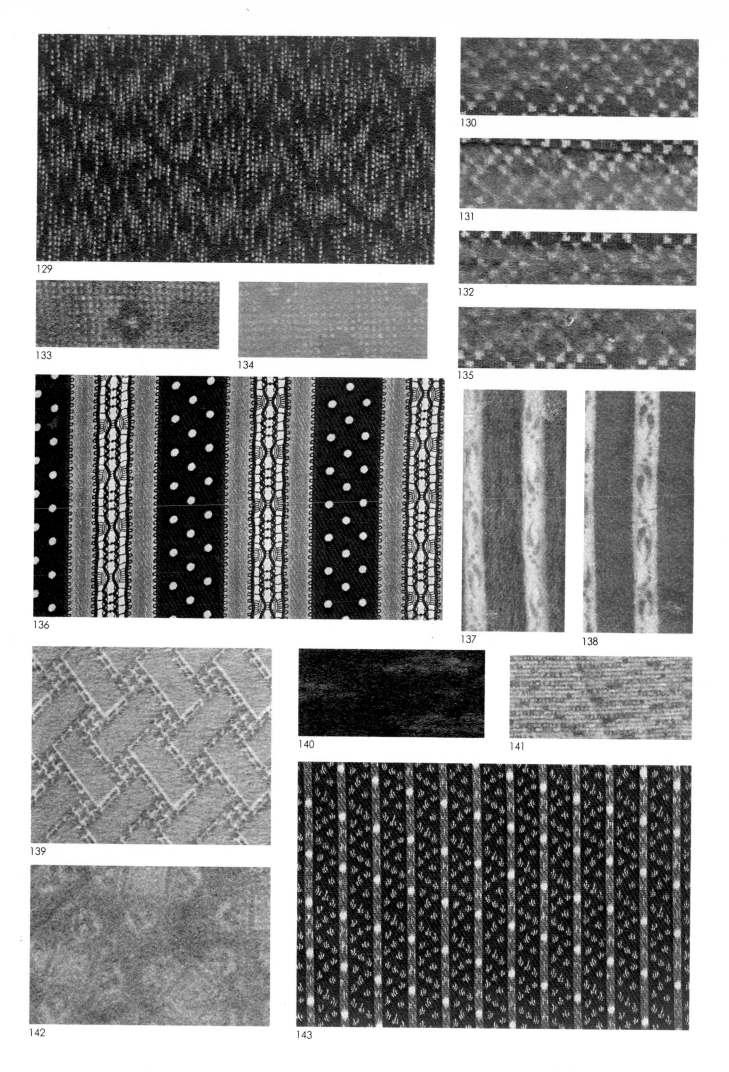

129

130

131

132

133

134

135

136

137

138

139

140

141

142

143

55

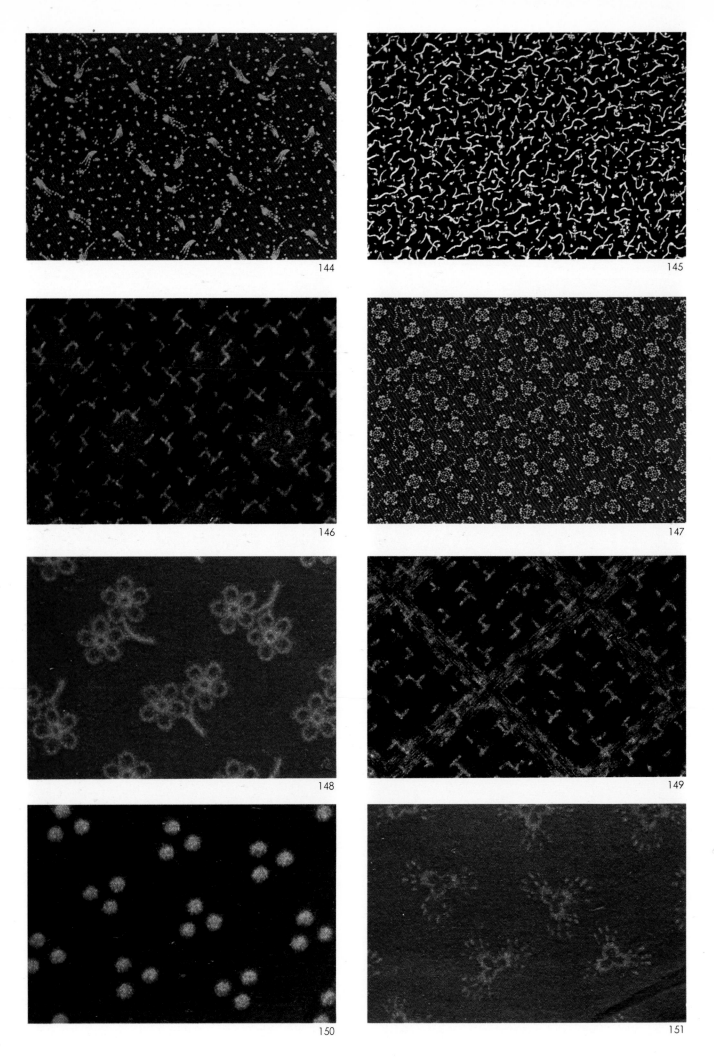

144

145

146

147

148

149

150

151

152

153

154

155

156

157

158

159

160

161

162

163

164

165

166

167

168

169

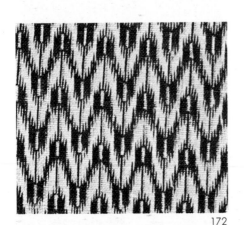

170

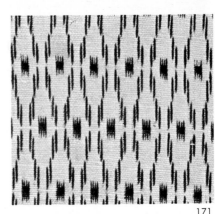

171

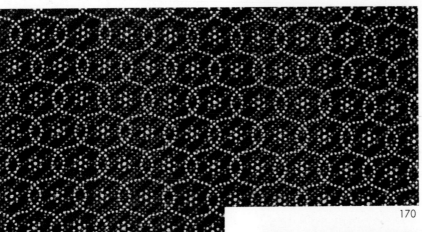

172

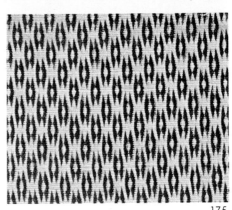

173

174

175

176

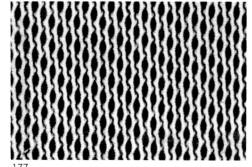

177

179

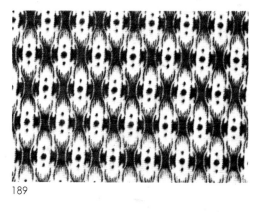

178

180

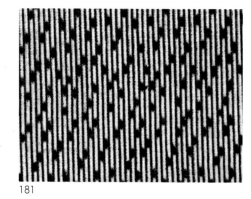

181

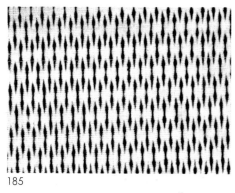

181

182

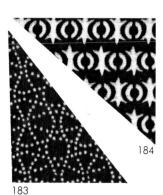

183

184

185

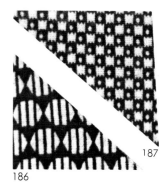

186

187

188

189

190

191

192

193

194

195

196

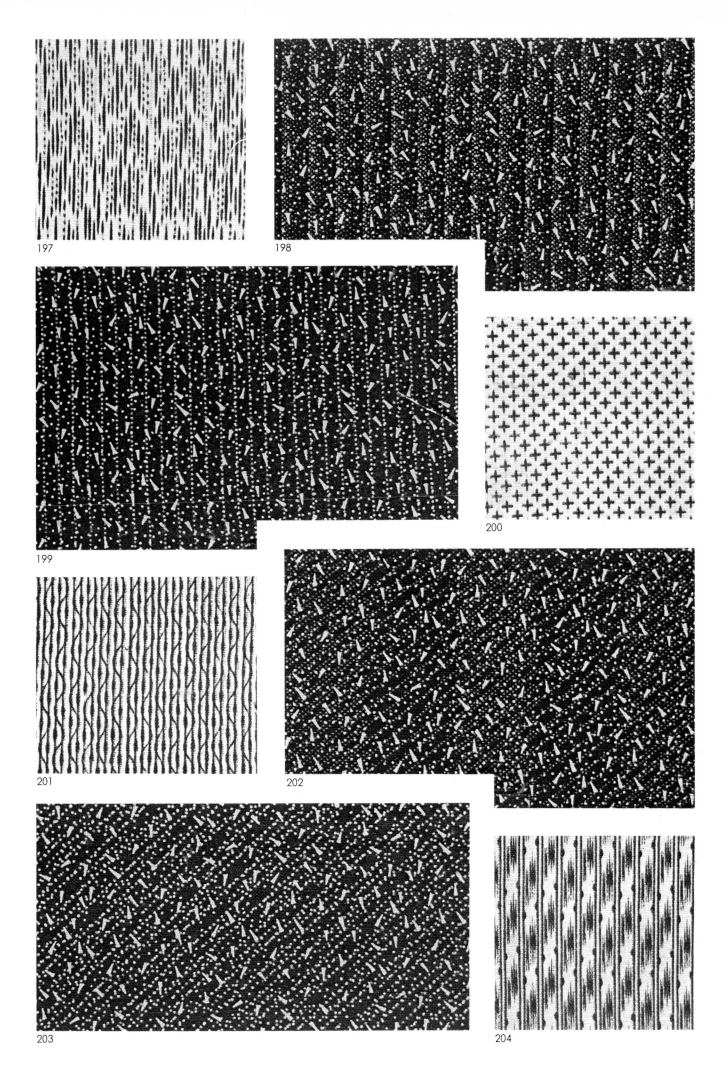

197

198

199

200

201

202

203

204

205

206

207

208

209

210

211

212

213

214

215

216

217

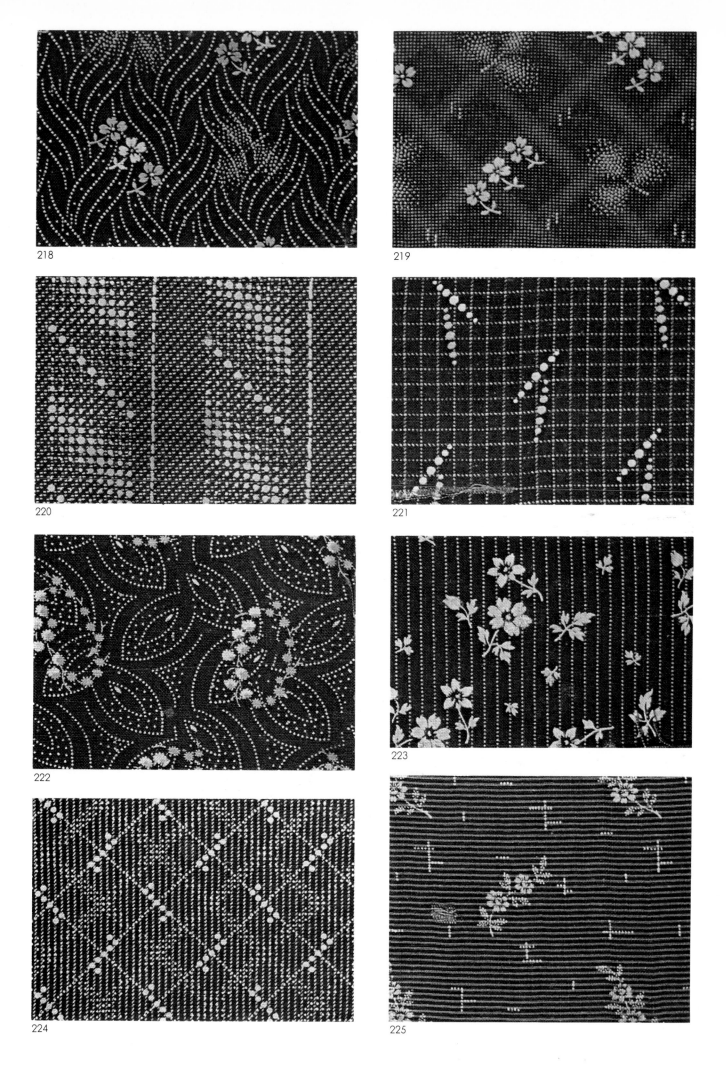

218

219

220

221

222

223

224

225

226

227

228

229

230

231

232

233

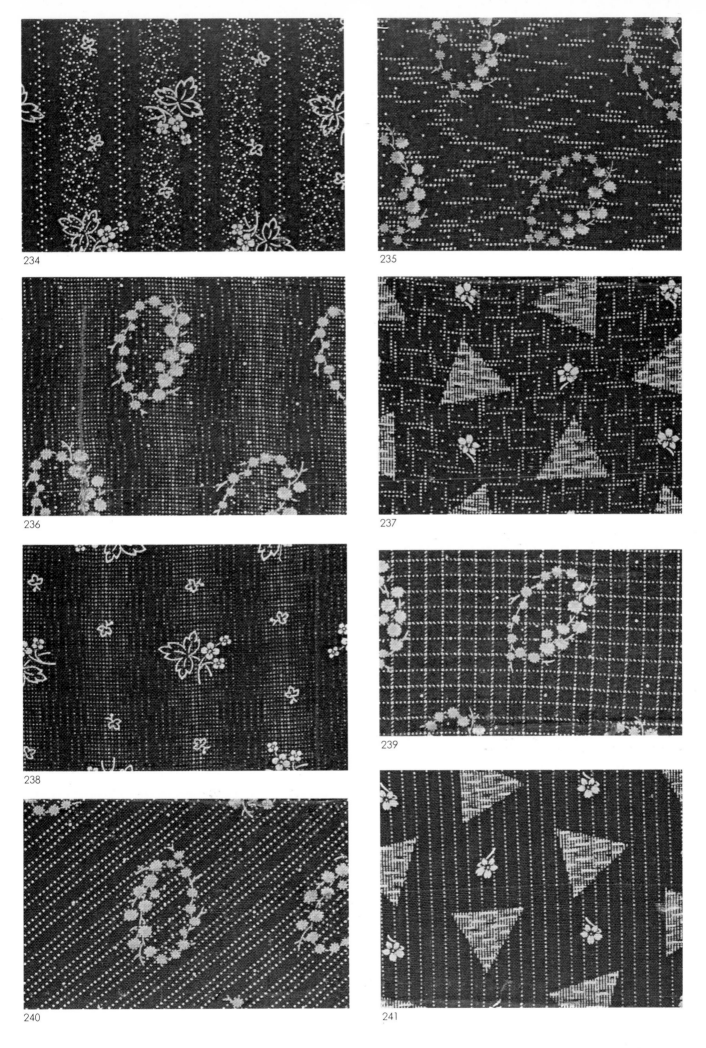

234

235

236

237

238

239

240

241

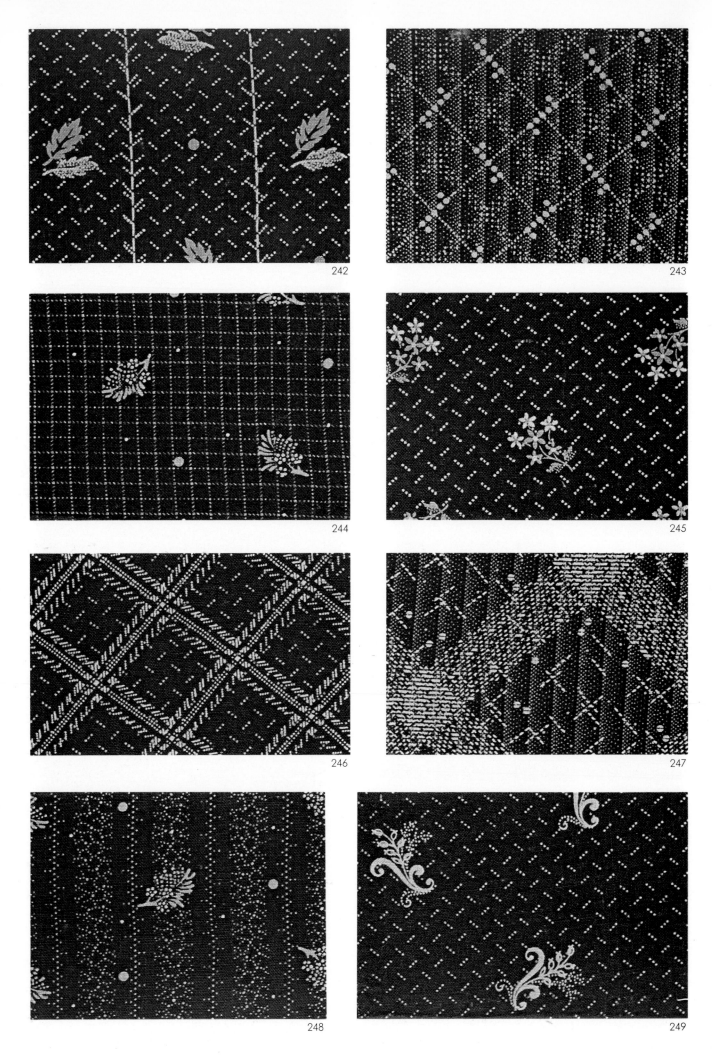

242

243

244

245

246

247

248

249

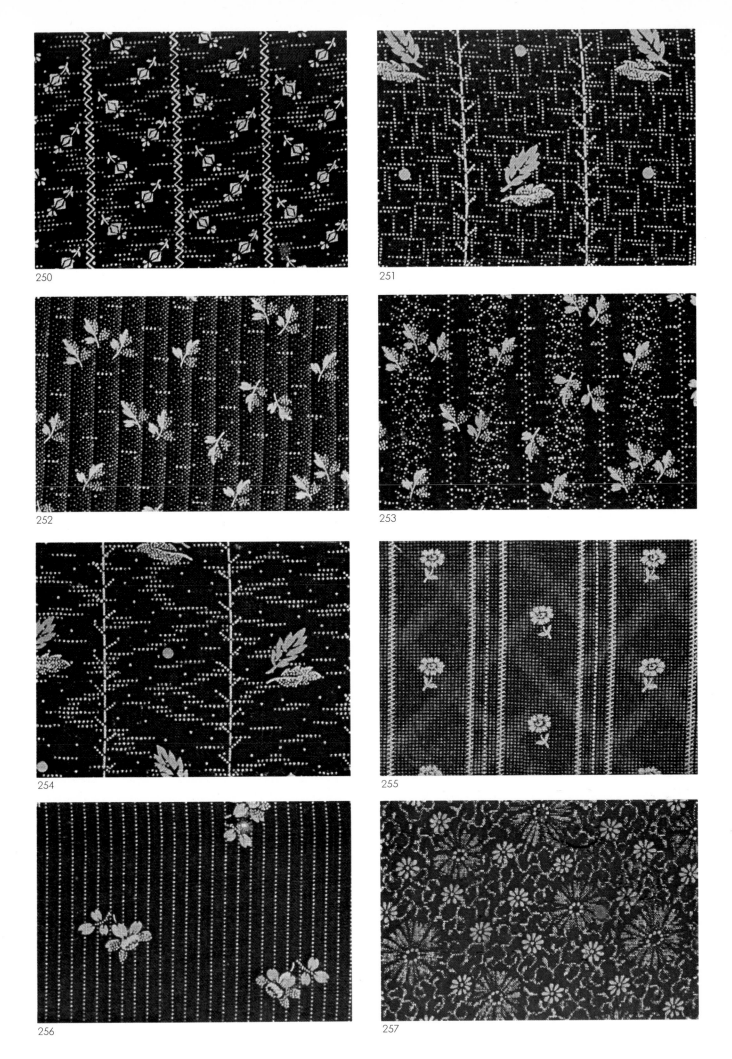

250

251

252

253

254

255

256

257

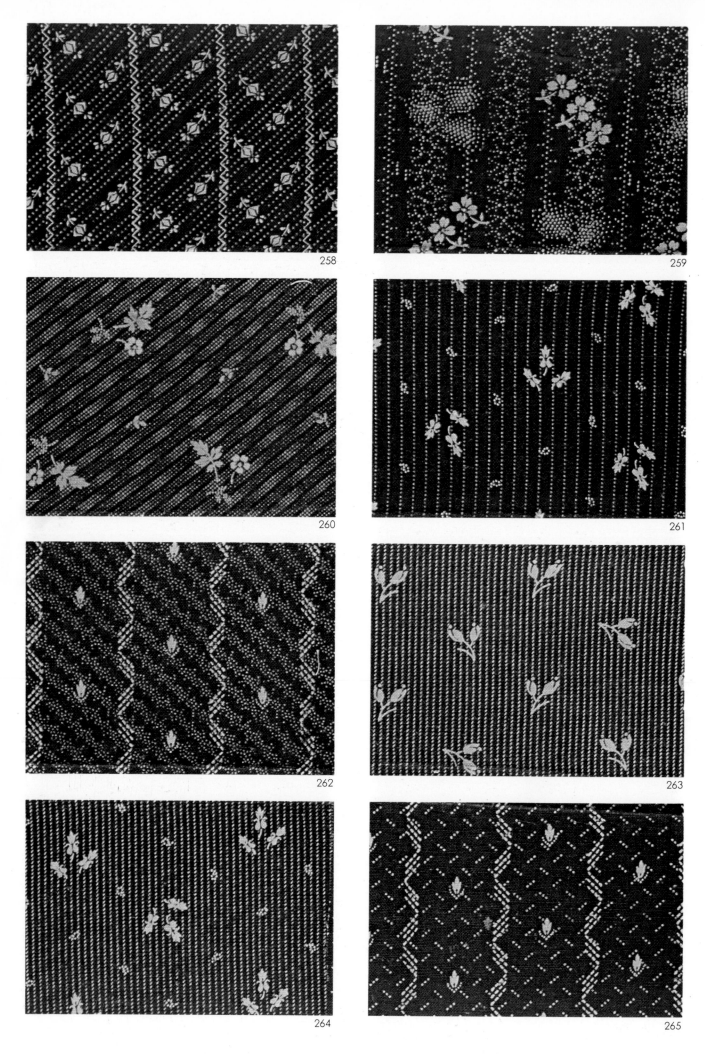

258

259

260

261

262

263

264

265

266

267

268

269

270

271

272

273

274

275

276

277

278

279

280

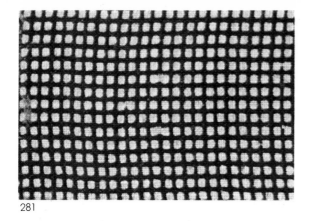

281

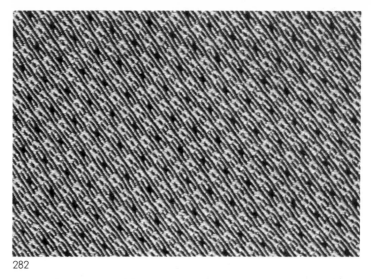

282

283

284

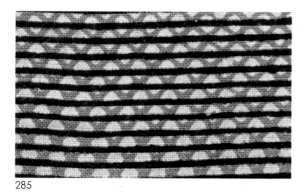

285

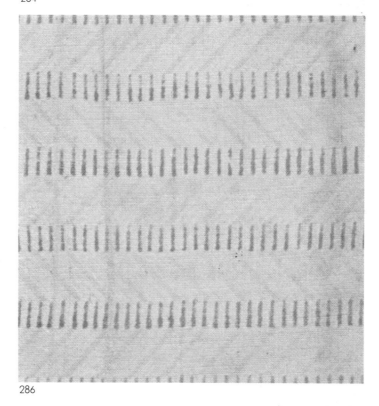

286

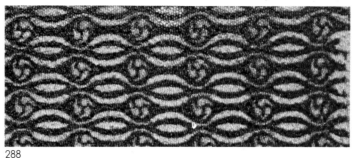

287

288

289

290

291

292

293

294

295

296

297

298

299

300

301

302

303

304

305

306

307

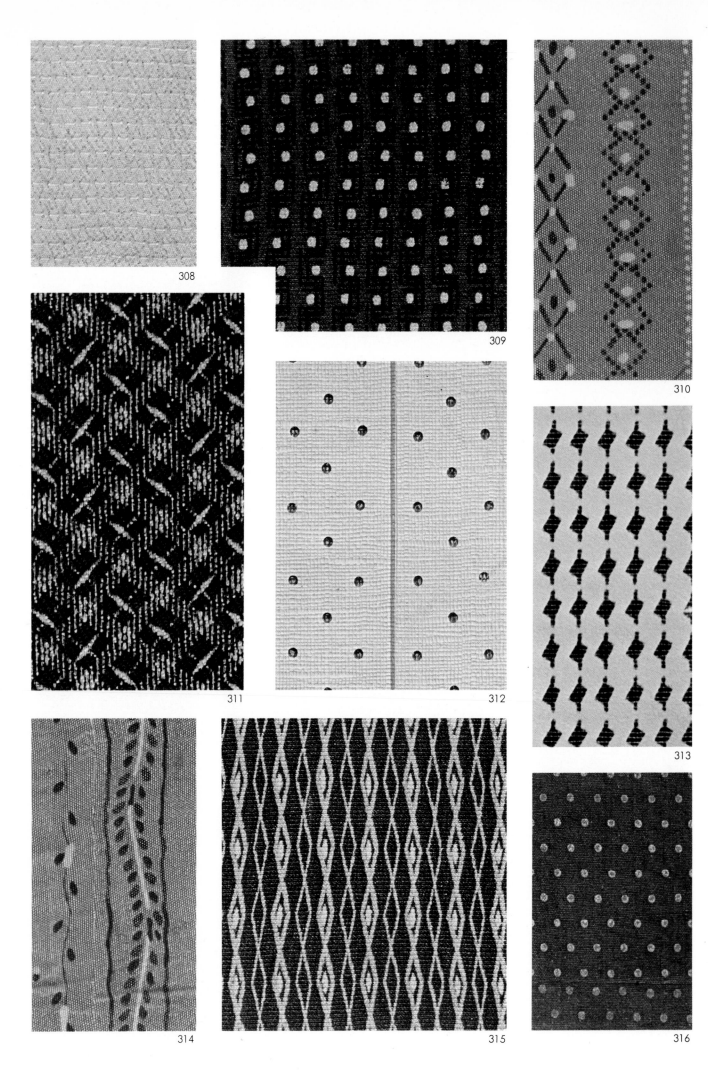

308

309

310

311

312

313

314

315

316

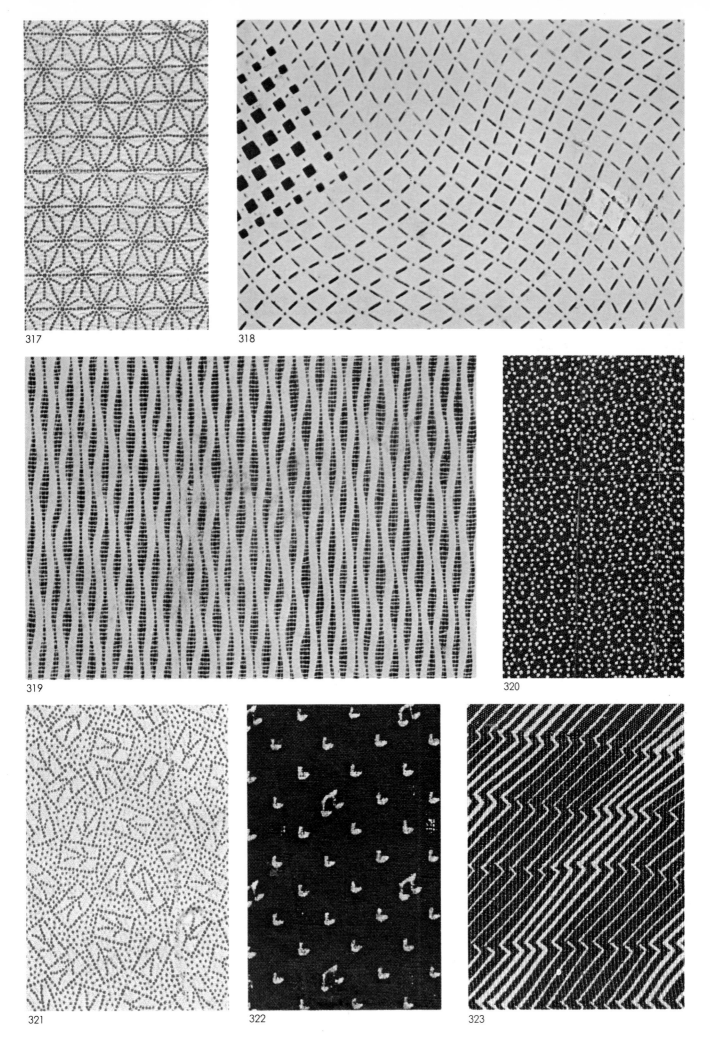

317

318

319

320

321

322

323

324

325

326

327

328

329

330

331

332

333

334

335

336

337

338

339

340

341

342

343

344

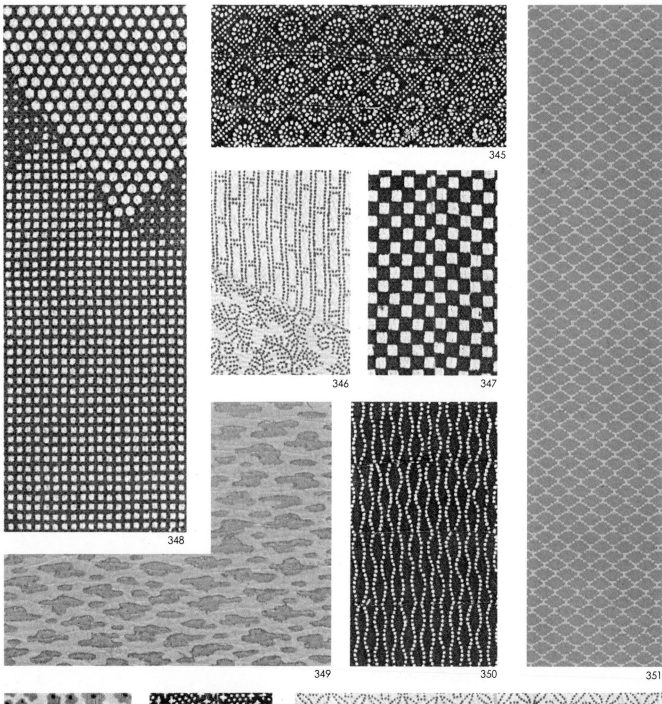

345

346 347

348

349 350 351

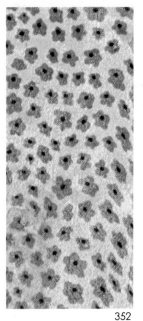

352

353 354

355

356

357

358

359

360

361

362

363

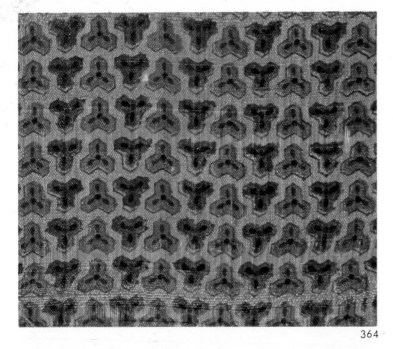

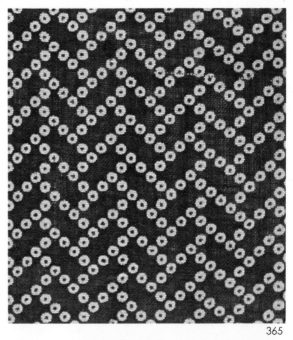

364

365

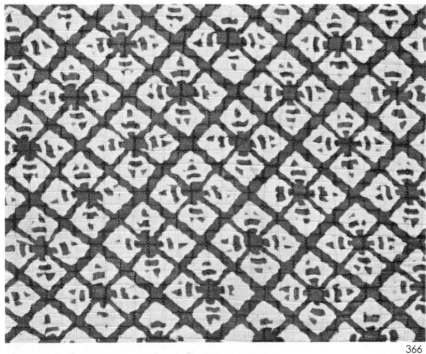

366

367

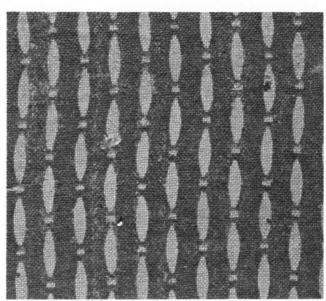

368

369

Arts and crafts paper
(small motif)

Bastelpapier
(kleines Muster)

Papier dessin
(petit motif)

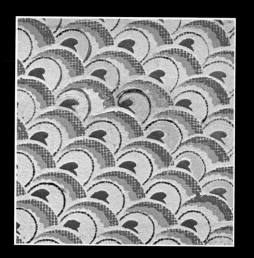

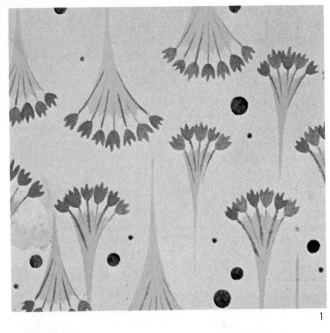

1

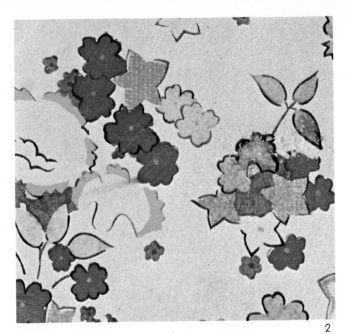

2

3

4

5

6

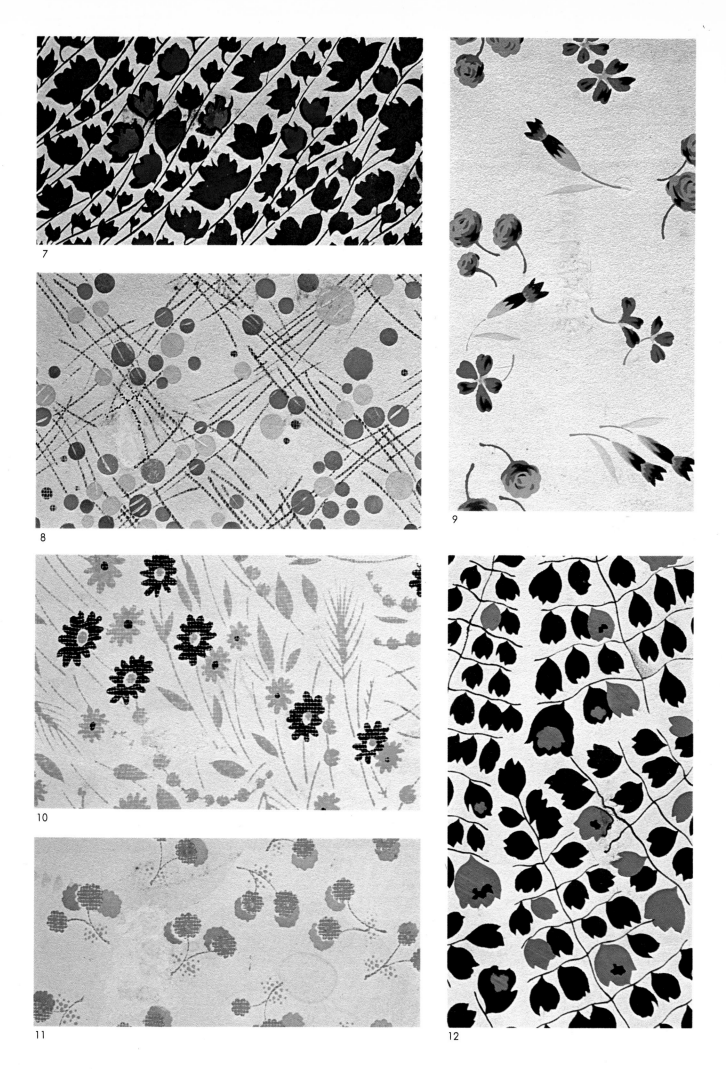

7

8

9

10

11

12

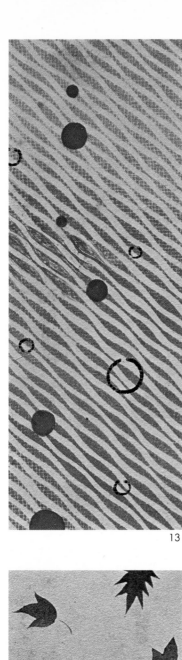

13

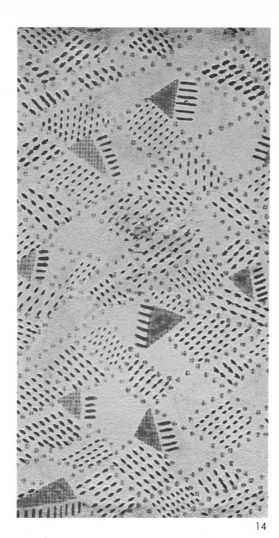

14

15

16

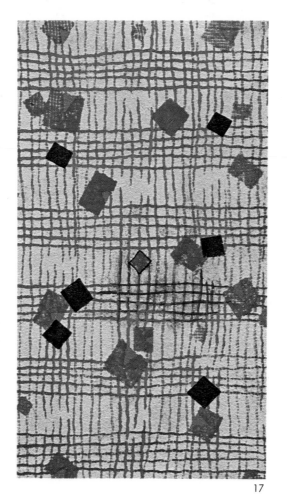

17

18

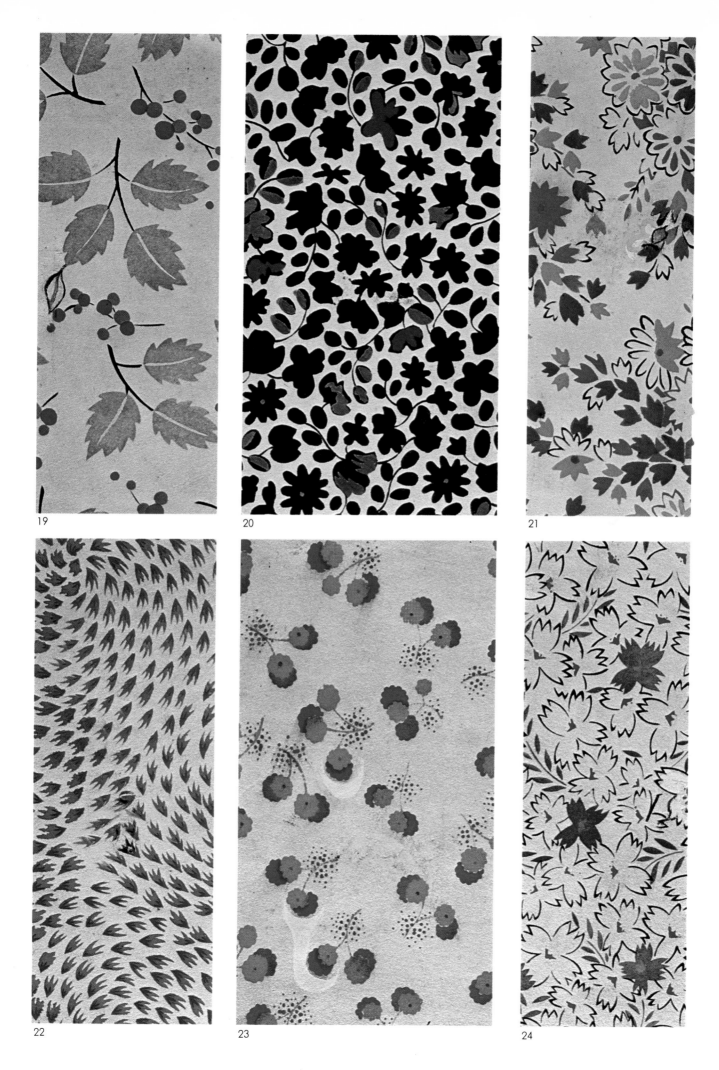

19

20

21

22

23

24

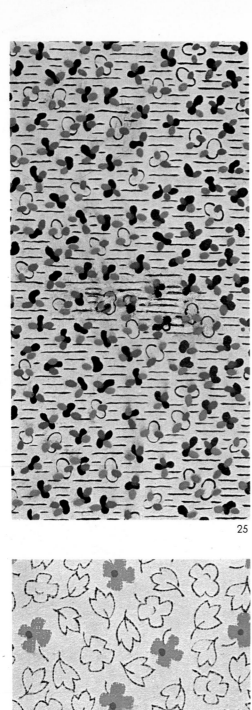

25

26

27

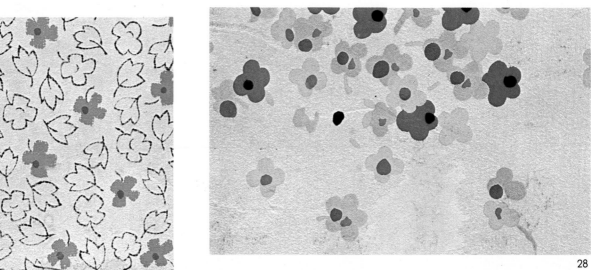

28

29

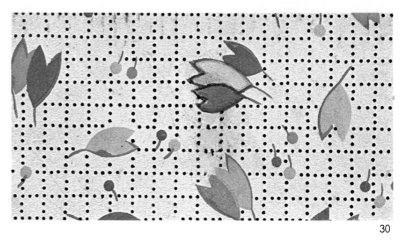

30

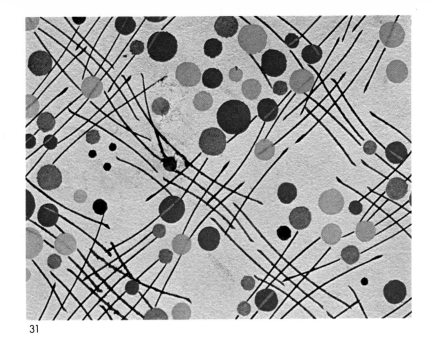

31

32

33

34

35

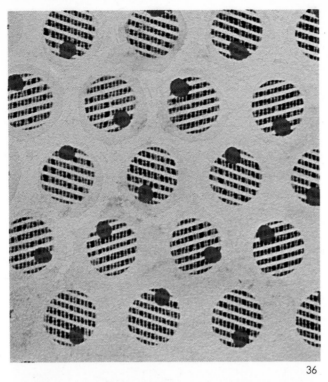

36

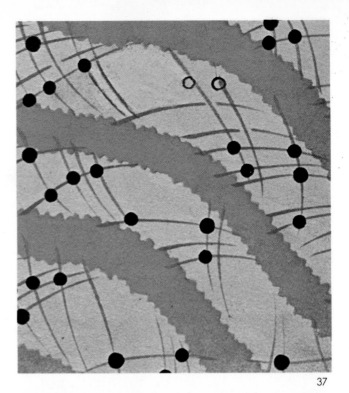

37

38

39

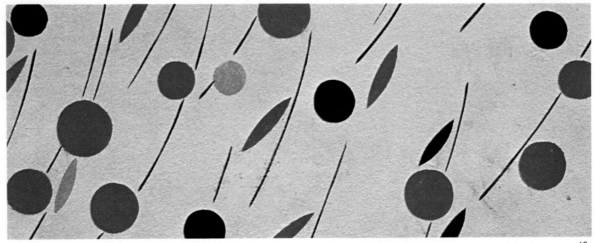

40

41

42

43

44

45

46

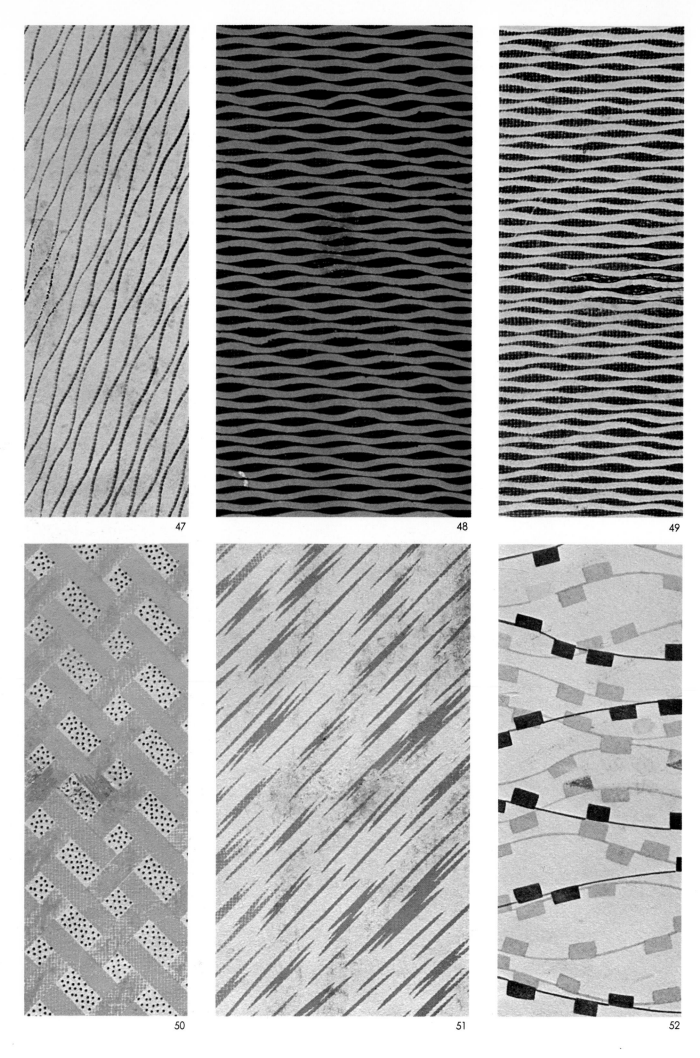

47

48

49

50

51

52

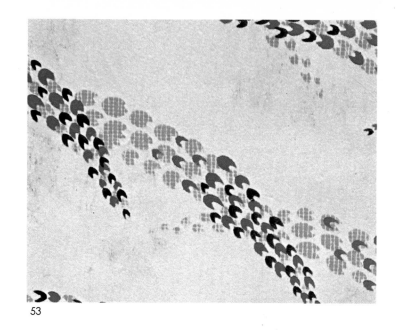

53

54

55

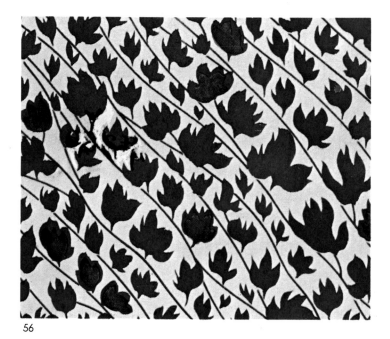

56

57

58

59

60

61

62

63

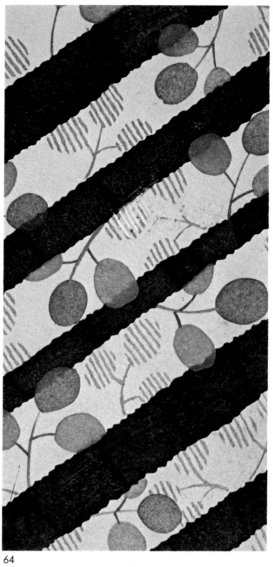

64

65

66

67

68

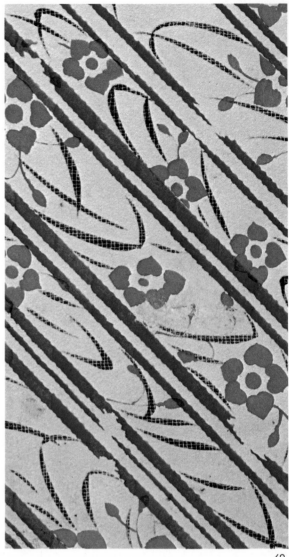

69

70

71

72

CHUGATA patterns
(medium-sized motifs) of the Meiji and Taisho periods (cloth)

CHUGATA - Muster
(mittelgroße Muster) aus der Meidschi- und Taishozeit (Stoff)

Motifs CHUGATA
(motifs de taille moyenne) des ères Meiji et Taisho (tissu)

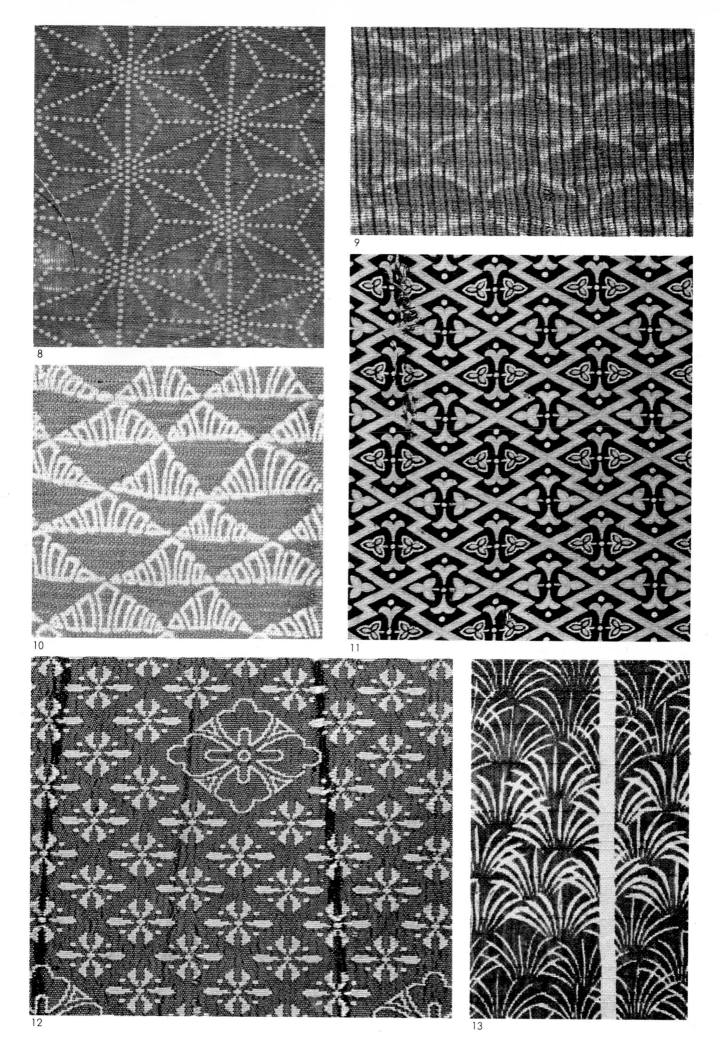

14

15

16

17

18

19

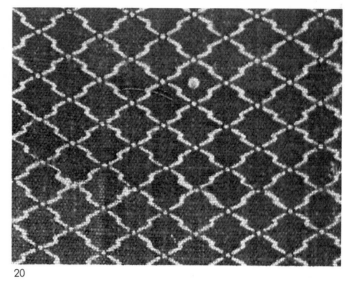

20

21

22

23

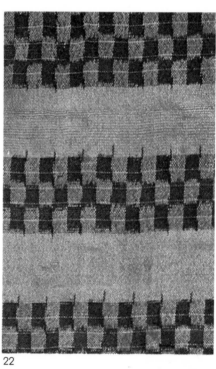

24

25

27

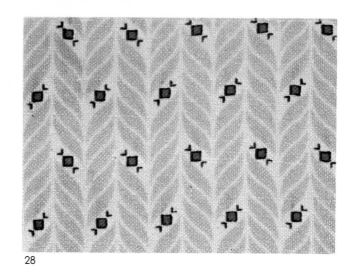

28

29

30

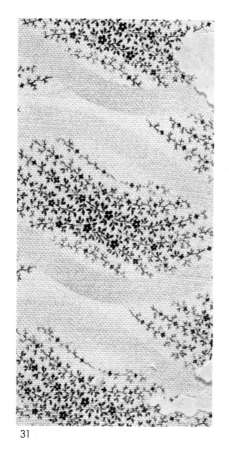

31

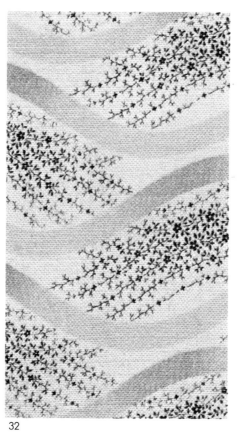

32

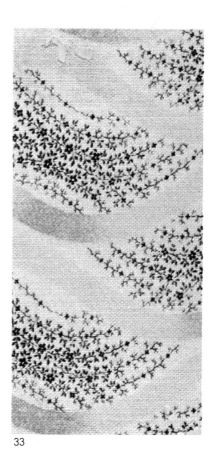

33

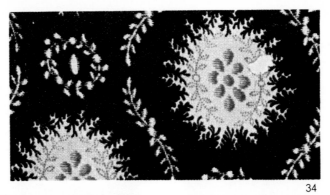

34

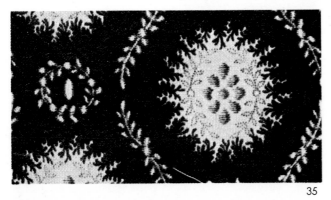

35

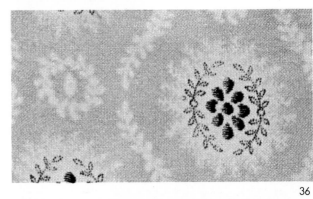

36

37

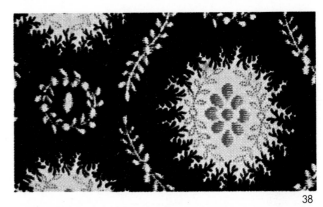

38

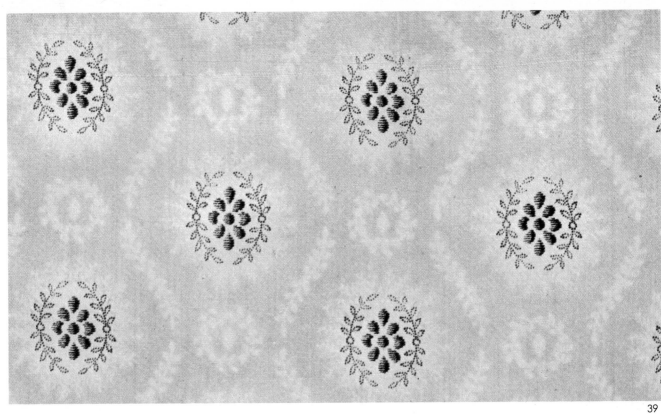

39

40

41

42

43

44

45

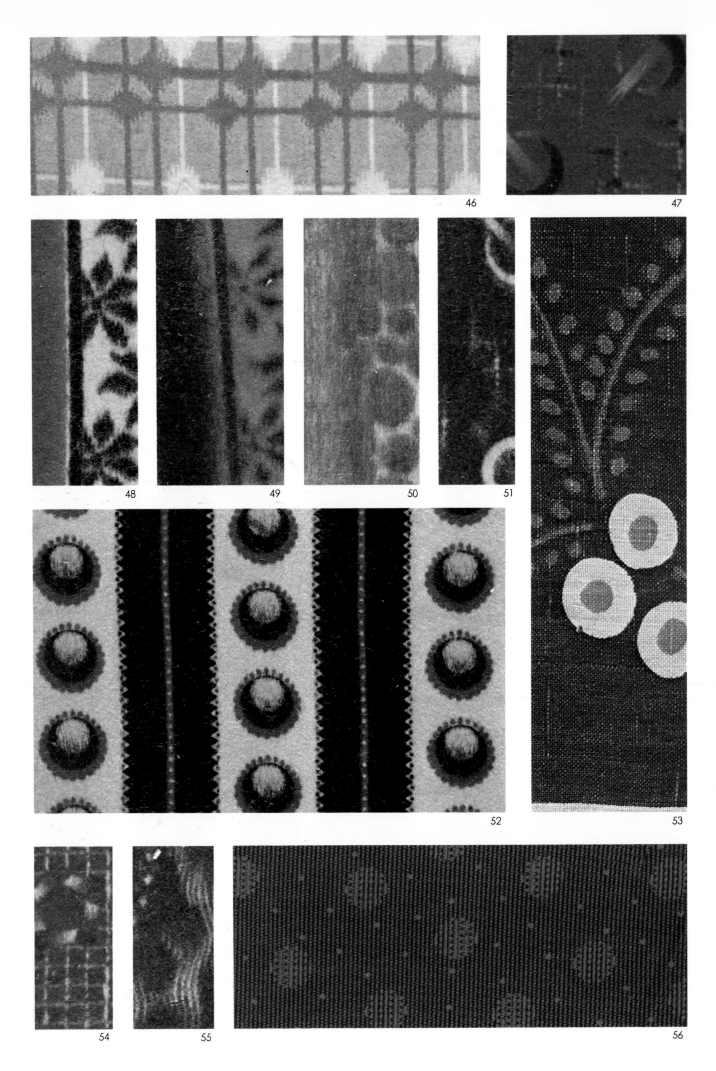

46

47

48

49

50

51

52

53

54

55

56

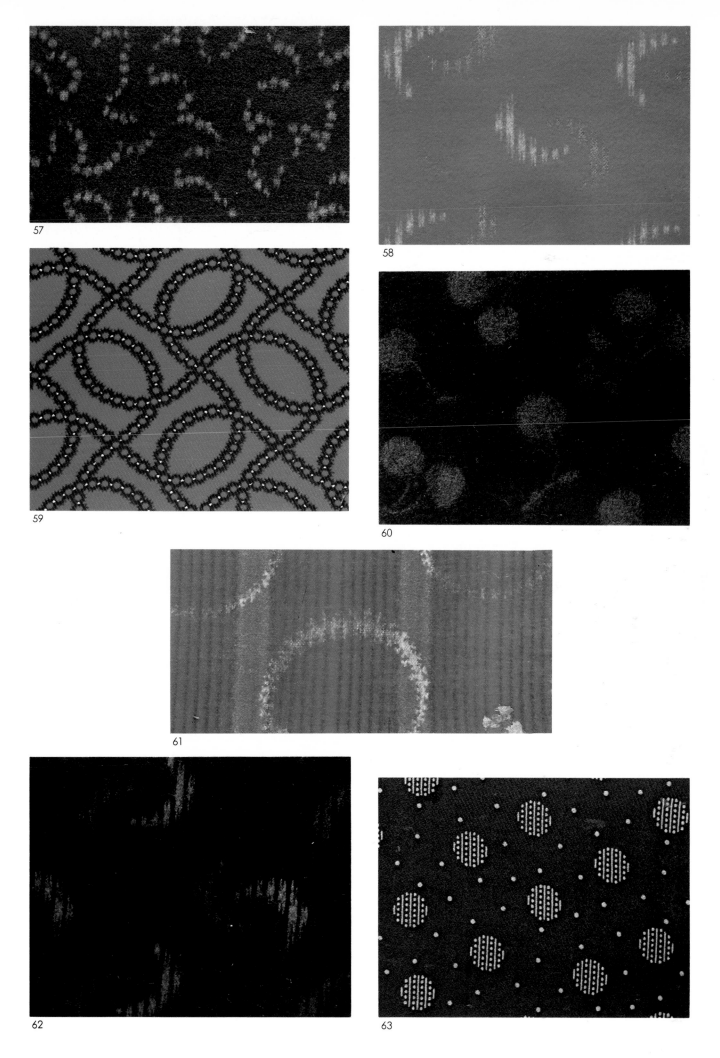

57

58

59

60

61

62

63

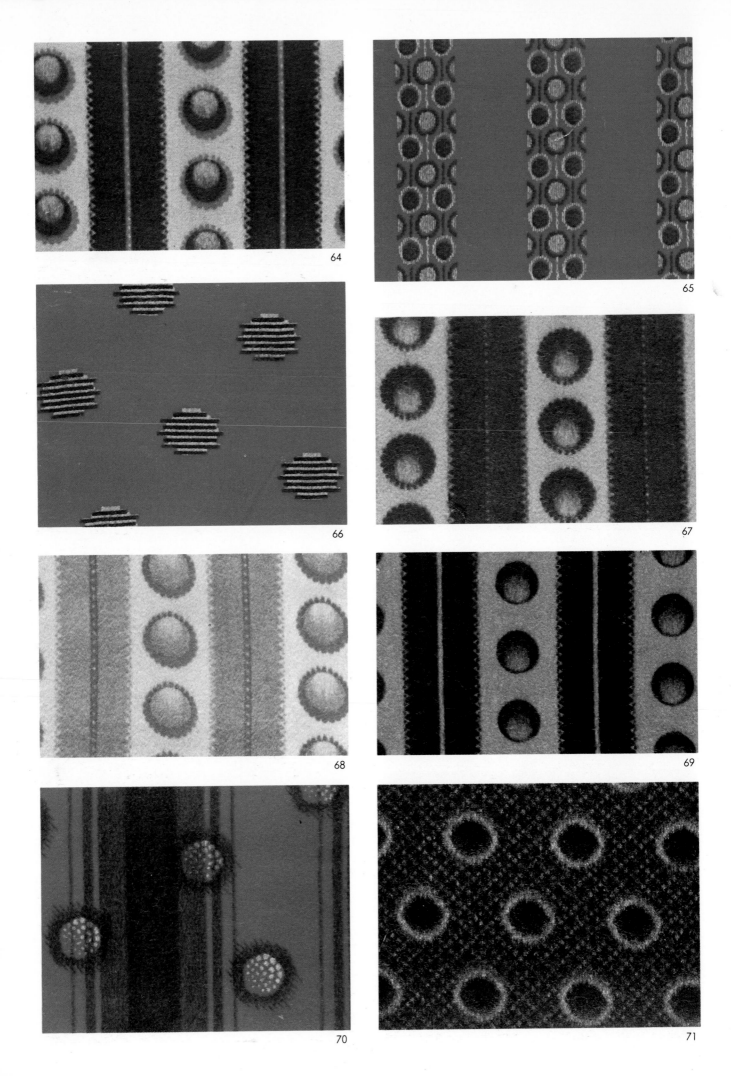

72

73

74

75

76

77

78

79

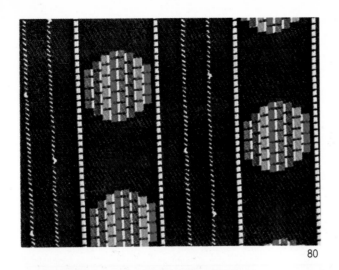

80

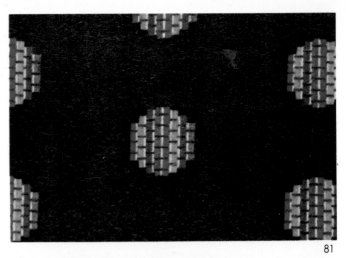

81

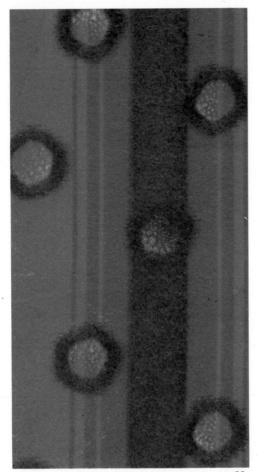

83

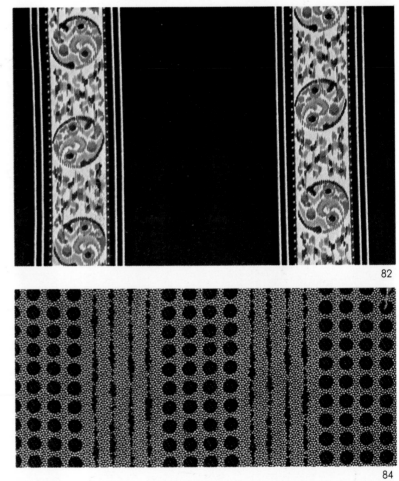

82

84

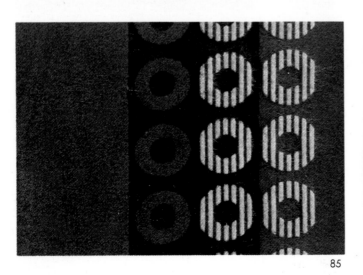

85

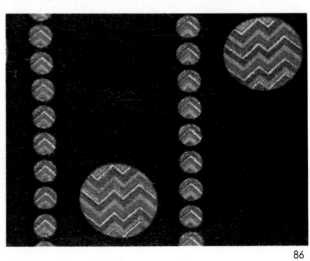

86

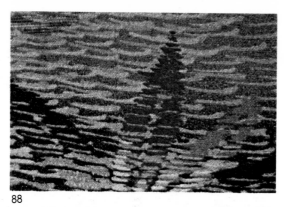

87

88

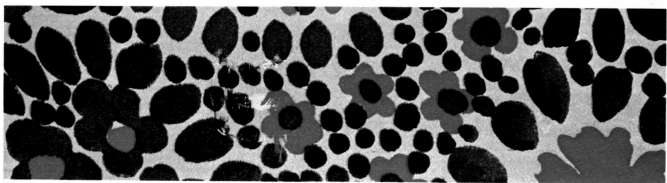

89

90

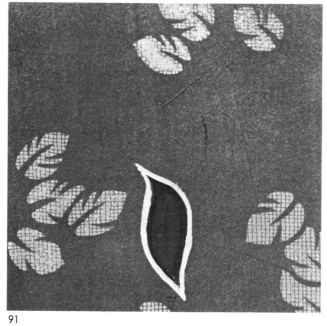

91

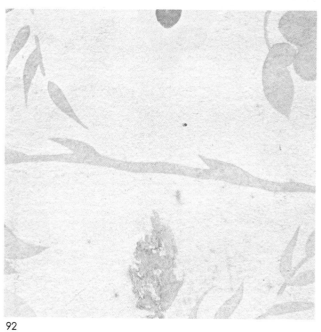

92

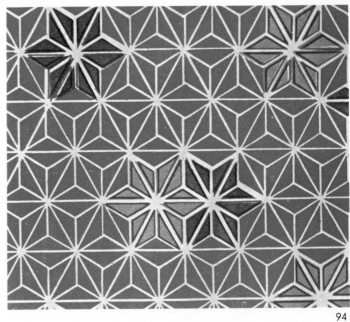

93

94

95

96

97

98

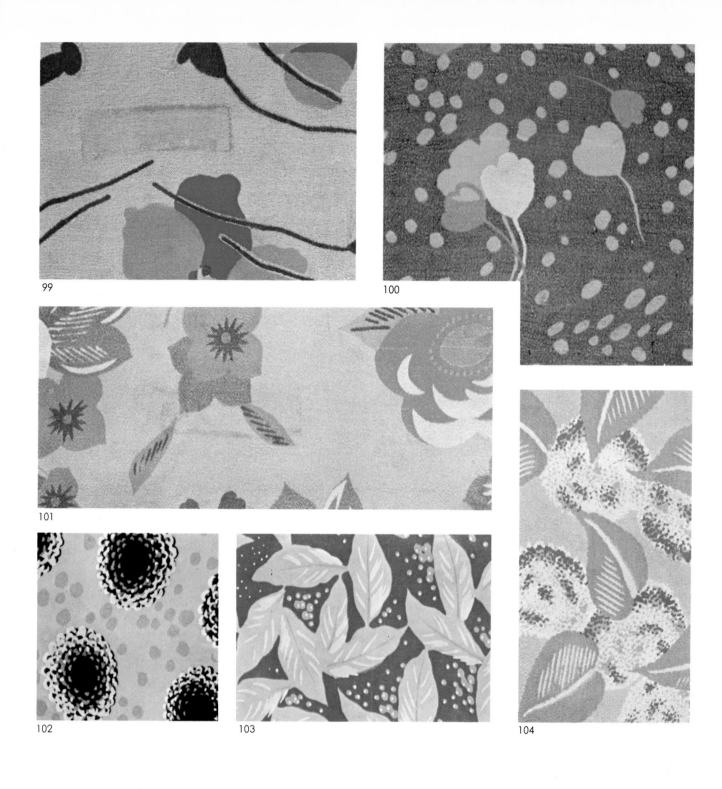

99

100

101

102

103

104

105

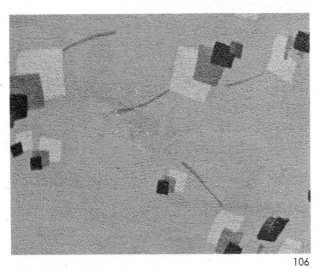

106

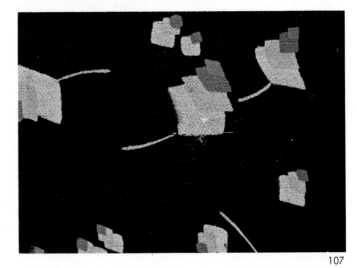

107

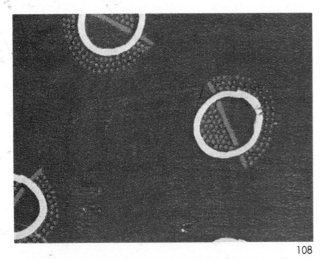

108

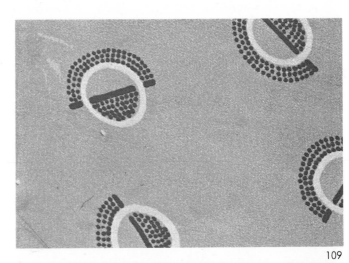

109

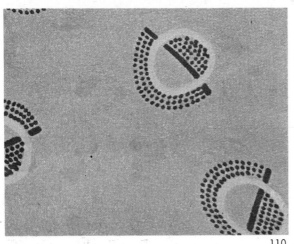

110

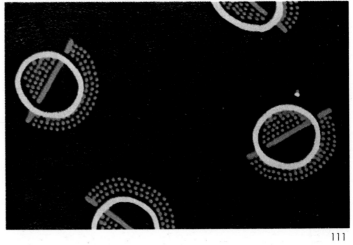

111

5

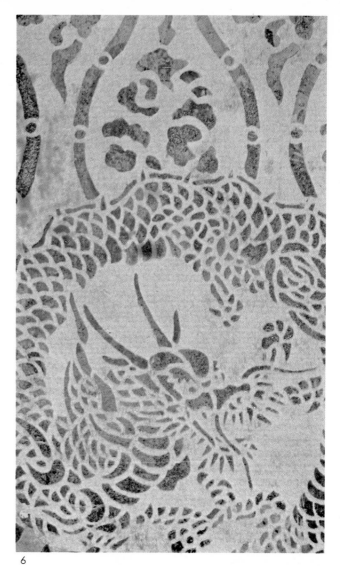

6

7

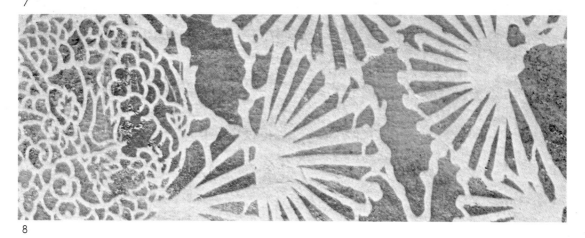

8

9

10

11

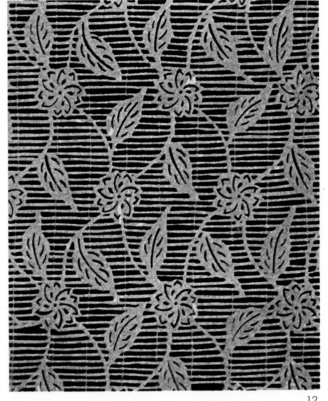

12

13

14

15

16

17

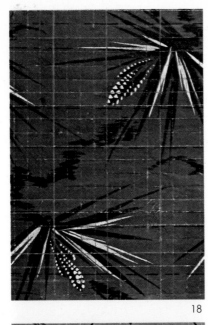

18

19

20

21

22

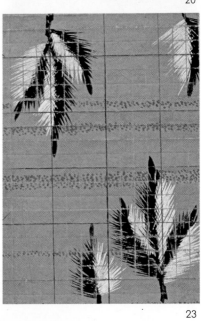

23

24

25

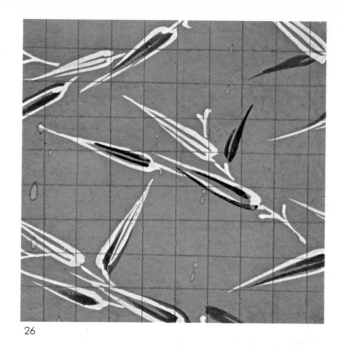

26

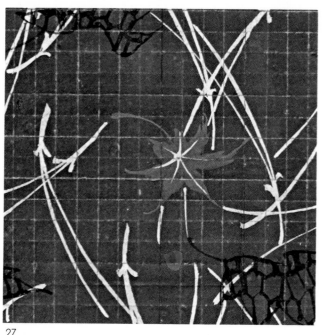

27

28

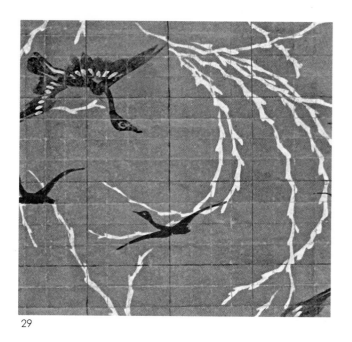

29

30

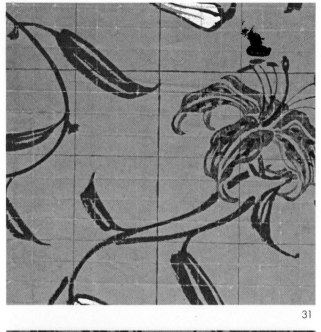

31

32

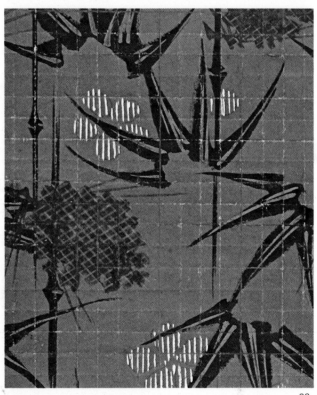

33

34

35

36

37

38

39

40

41

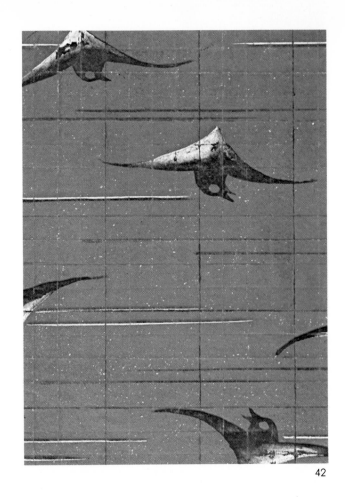

42

43

44

45

46

47

48

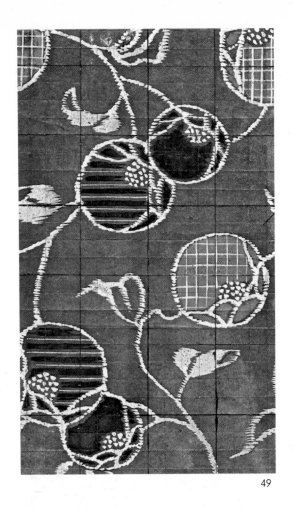

49

50

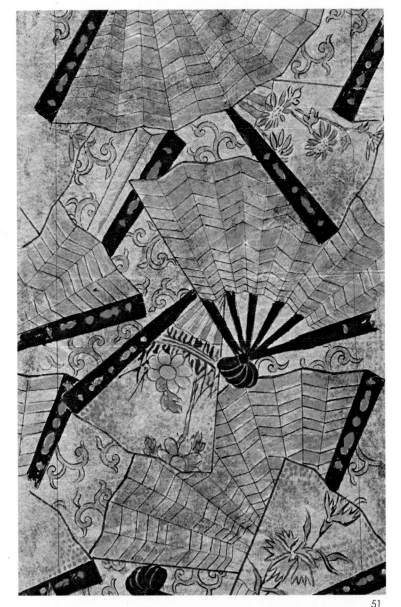

51

52

53

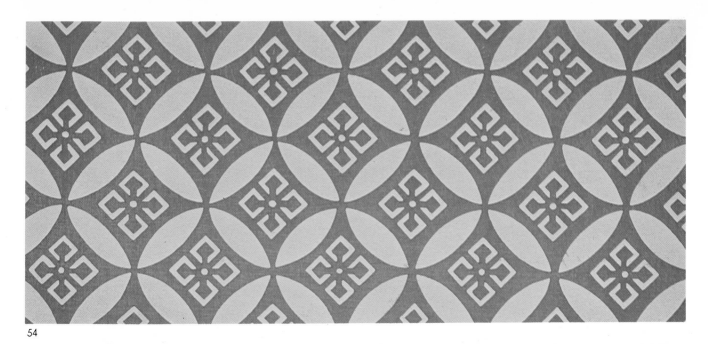

54

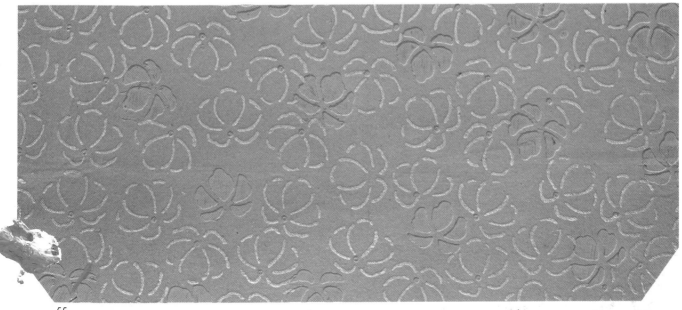

55

56

57

58

59

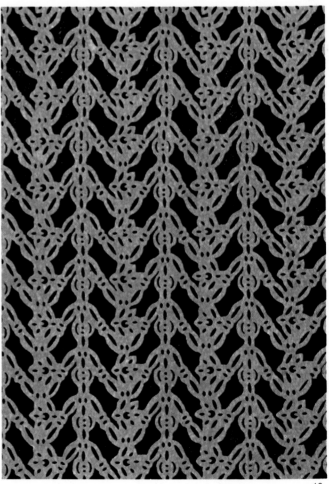

60

61

62

63

64

65

66

67

68

69

70

71

72

73

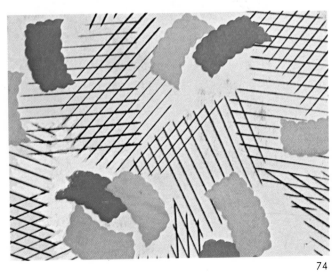

74

75

76

77

78

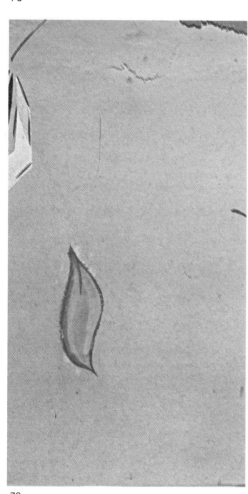

79

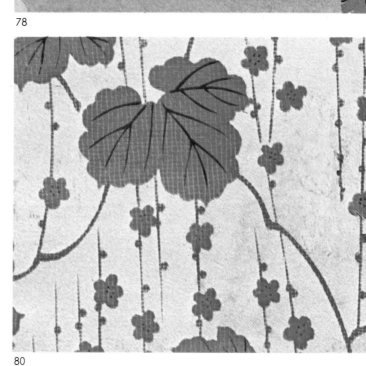

80

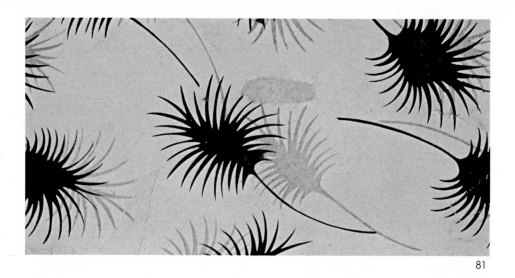

81

82

83

84

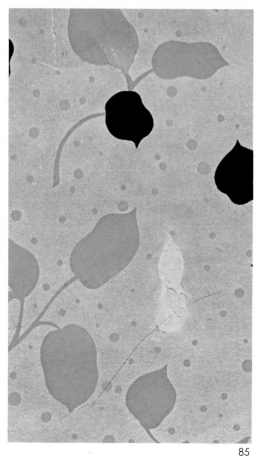

85

86

87

88

89

90

91

92

93

94

95

96

97

98

99

100

101

102

103

104

105

106

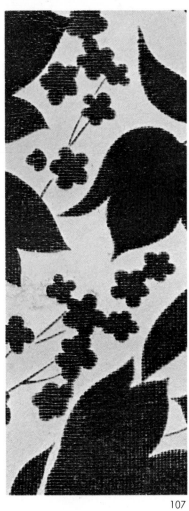

107

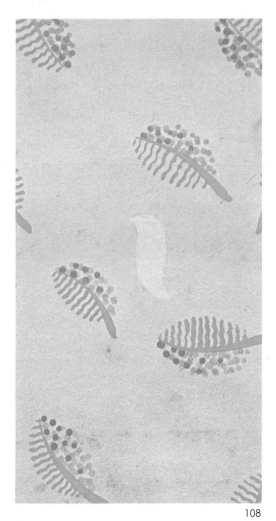

108

109

110

111

112

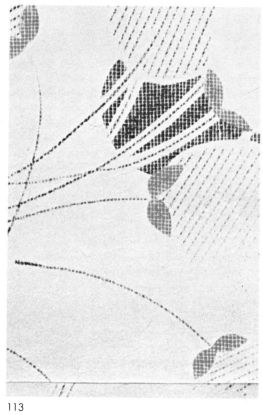

113

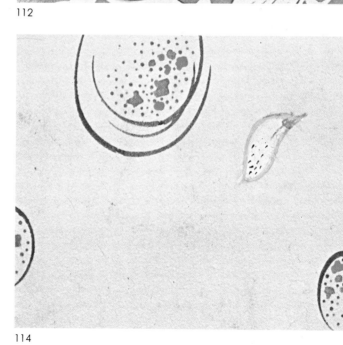

114

115

116

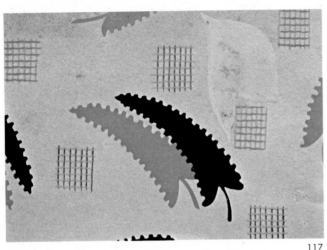

117

118

119

120

121

122

123

124

125

126

127

128

129

130

131

132

133

134

135

136

137

138

139

140

141

142

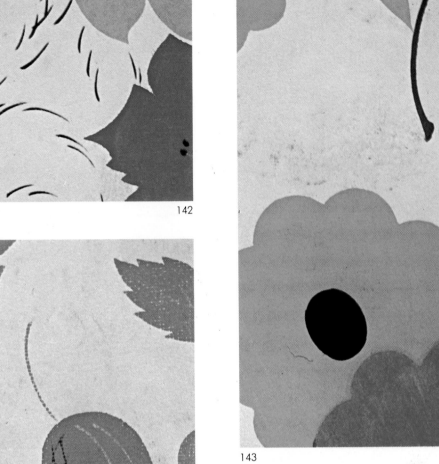

143

144

145

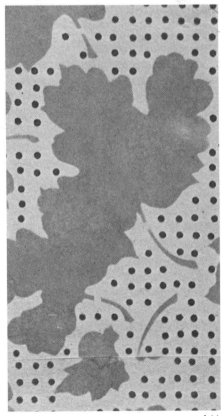

146

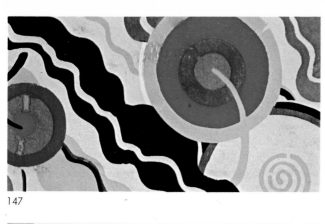

147

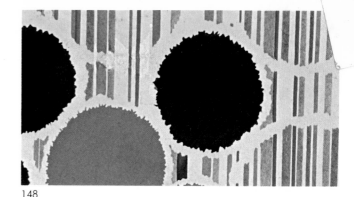

148

149

150

151

152

153

154

155

156

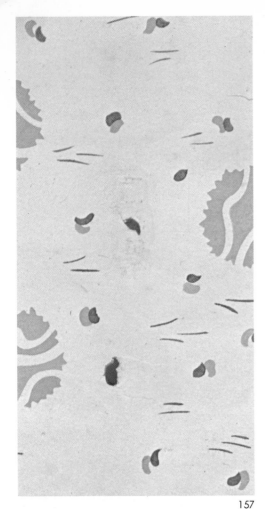

158

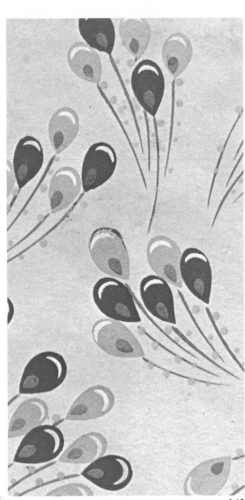

157

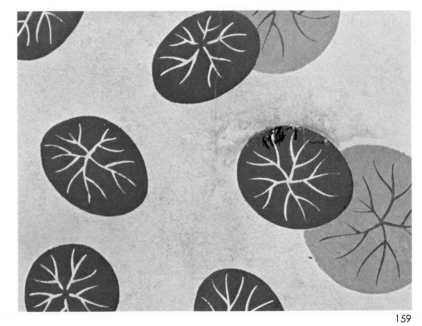

159

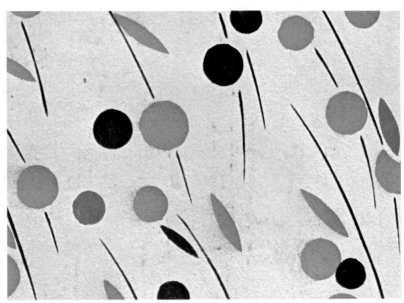

160

161

162

163

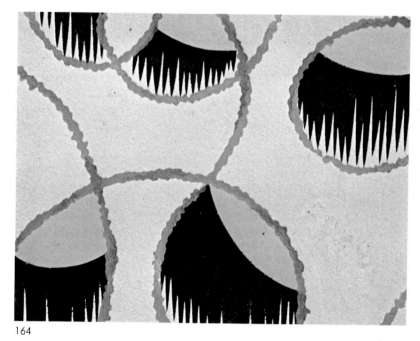

164

165

166

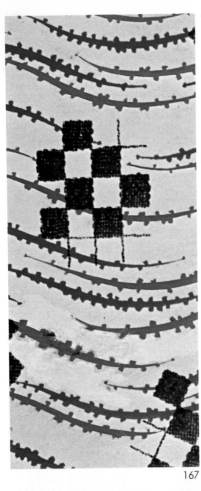

167

168

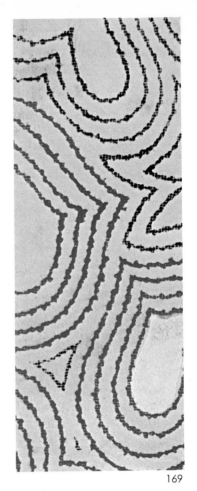

169

170

171

172

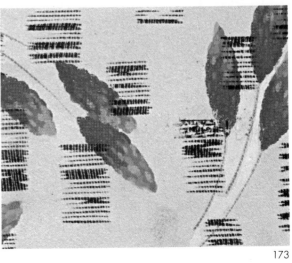

173

174

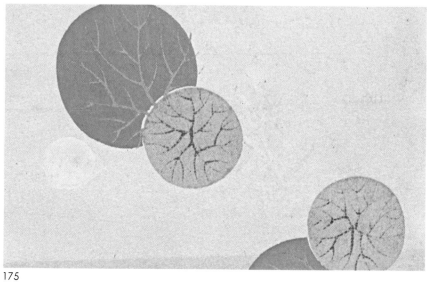

175

176

177

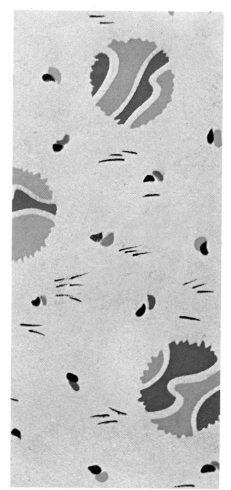

178

179

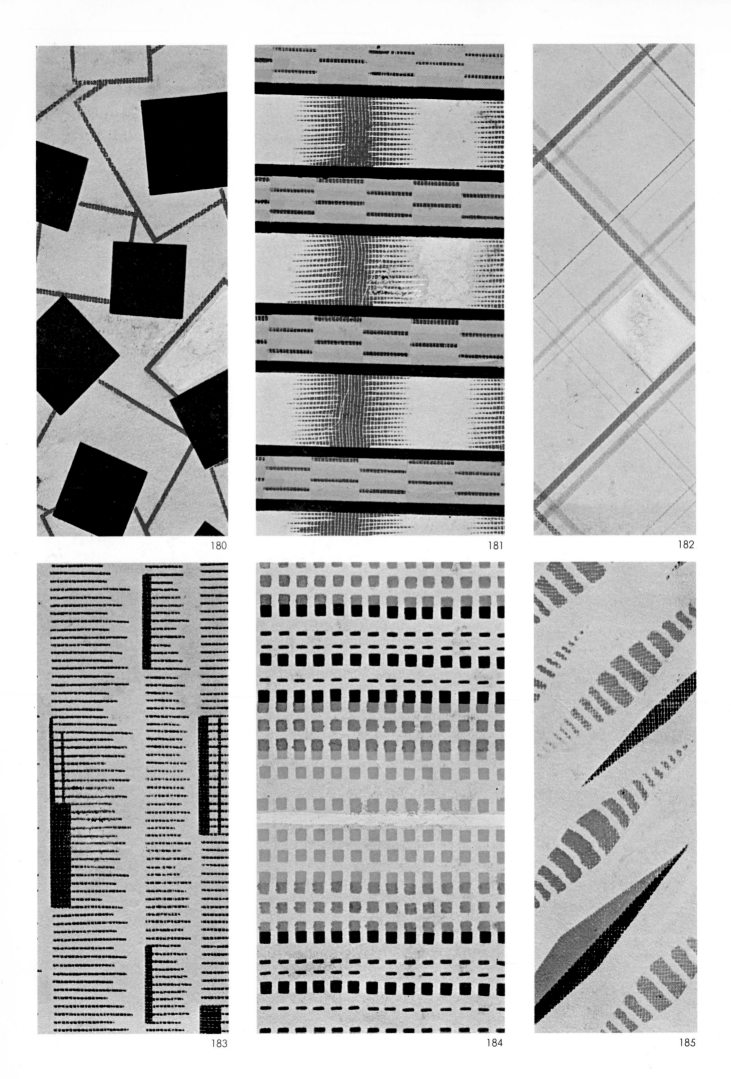

180   181   182

183   184   185

186

187

188

189

190

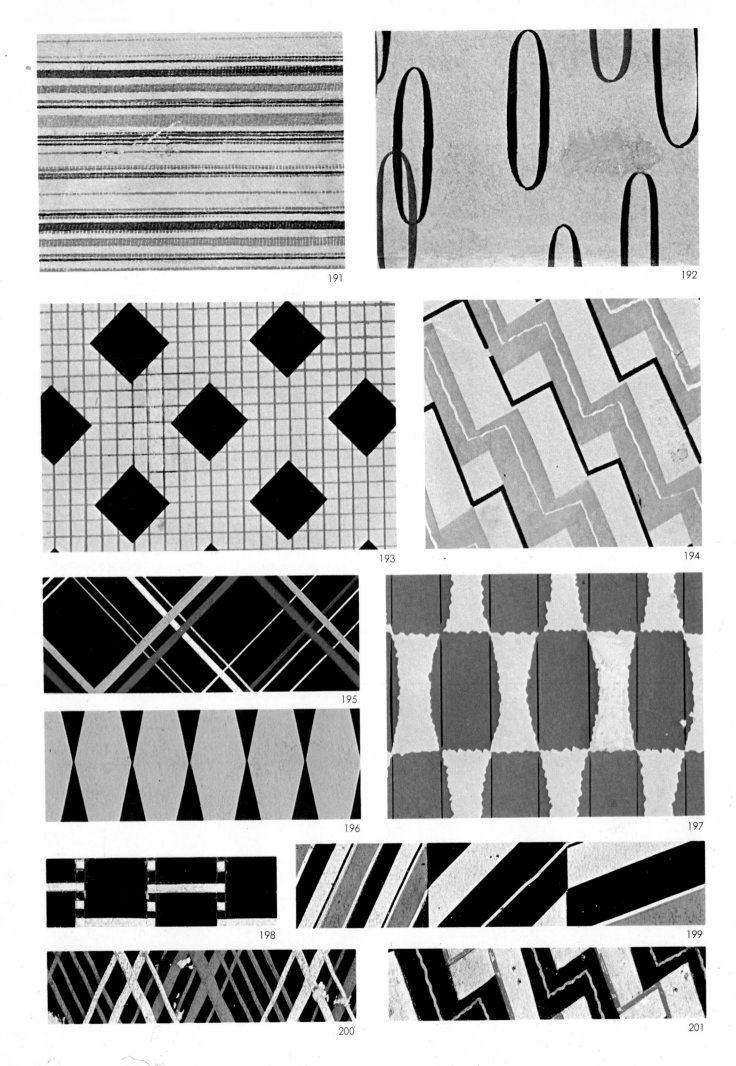

191

192

193

194

195

196

197

198

199

200

201

202

203

204

205

206

207

208

209

210

211

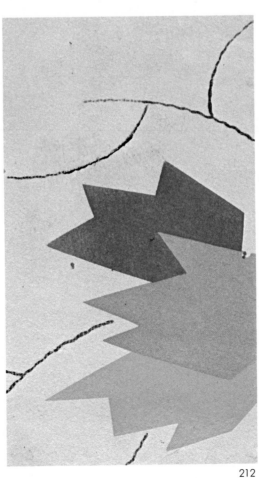

212

213

214

215

216

217

218

219

220

221

222

223

224

225

152

226

227

228

229

230

231

232

233

234

235

236

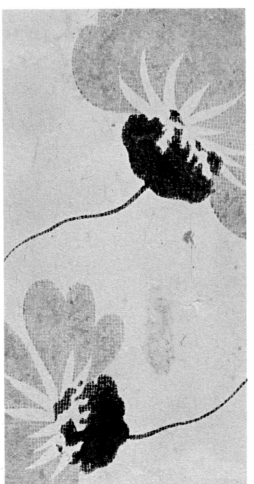

237

238

239

154